DIVING *in the* *Caribbean*

DIVING
in the Caribbean

LAWSON WOOD

RIZZOLI
NEW YORK

First published in the
United States of America in 1998 by
RIZZOLI INTERNATIONAL PUBLICATIONS, INC.
300 Park Avenue South, New York, NY 10010

First published in Great Britain in 1998 by
New Holland (Publishers) Ltd
London • Cape Town • Sydney • Singapore

ISBN 0-8478-2132-3
LC 98-65887

SENIOR DESIGNER **TRINITY LOUBSER-FRY**
EDITORS **JANE MALIEPAARD** AND **THEA GROBBELAAR**
PUBLISHING MANAGER **MARIËLLE RENSSEN**
DTP CARTOGRAPHER **JOHN LOUBSER**
DESIGN ASSISTANT **SIMON LEWIS**
CONSULTANT **DR PHIL HEEMSTRA**
PICTURE RESEARCHER **CARMEN WATTS**
INDEXER **BRENDA BRICKMAN**

Reproduction by
UNIFOTO (PTY) LTD

Printed and bound in Singapore by
TIEN WAH PRESS (PTE) LTD

CONTENTS

I enjoyed some of my greatest Caribbean dive adventures during 1997, the International Year of the Reef. The most exotic dive involved steadying myself above the bridge of a Russian frigate while she sank to the bottom of the sea. As a young boy growing up in the south of France, I always experienced a degree of concern as my dad left for another expedition, knowing that if there were a problem on *Calypso*, it was the captain's responsibility – or at least tradition – to go down with the ship. I didn't want to lose my dad and the issue remained with me for many years. So when I was invited to film the Cayman Island's sinking of this ship for a new artificial reef, I decided to resolve the concern which had lingered for so many years during my youth. There I was, fitted out in dive equipment and standing on a ship, waiting for it to sink beneath my feet. I had made the decision to go down with the ship! As the frigate began to list and slip below, I had some second thoughts about my judgement, but the cameras were rolling and I was committed. When the chaos of turbulence and foam subsided, I found myself alone, serenely swimming among beautiful curtains of bubbles rising from the decks. The sun was setting and with the low light the scene was magnificent, but this was not what most impressed me about the frigate's sinking. The following day I returned to survey the 'reef' and found a small school of sergeant majors residing in the radar antenna, some squirrelfish and grunts around the propeller, a grouper midship and a barracuda guarding the bow. Amazing! This implement of death had become a source of life. Nature was already beginning to convert our weapon of destruction into a habitat for residents of this newest of Caribbean 'reefs'.

My other special experience involved bringing six children from France to the Bay Islands where we taught them to dive, and shared with them the wonders of coral reef ecology. We called them the 'Cyberkids' since they had brought with them digital still and video cameras and computers. Their objective was to share, through the Internet, their experiences and newly gained knowledge with students in a consortium of schools back in France. Every other day the live-aboard dive boat, the *Bay Islands Aggressor*, would return to port for the kids to send their images and descriptions back home. I was particularly impressed with the creativity, enthusiasm and sense of fun these young divers brought to the expedition. It reminded me why I have dedicated so much of my life to education and why I continue to work for the next generation. Having a certain degree of scepticism regarding electronic education, I was also impressed with how the technology had enabled the Cyberkids to produce some very creative works. In fact, these kids are now in production on a CD-ROM on coral-reef ecology and what it felt like to explore the beautiful reefs of the Bay Islands.

These two experiences reminded me of two very important issues. The fish inhabiting the sunken ship are an indication of the fantastic restorative capacity of nature. Coral reefs are under threat worldwide, but we cannot heal them ourselves. We can only cease the onslaught of human insult which undermines their health. The inherent vitality of nature will, in its own way, restore the magnificence of life on the stressed reefs. But this is dependent on our respecting these living jewels of the sea and preventing overfishing, destructive development and the release of nutrients and sediments which are presently killing them.

The Cyberkids reminded me that divers are very special people. Most humans have never, and will never, experience personally the wonders of the coral reef. In my opinion, this gives divers a very special status and some very important responsibilities. The kids who learned about reefs decided to share their experiences with students back home and even create a programme to educate others about these living structures. Like the Cyberkids, I believe all divers should be actively involved in the protection and wise management of reefs. They should be educators sharing with the nondiving public the beauty, fragility and need to protect them. Divers can participate in reef-monitoring programmes and actively lobby to implement marine protected areas, reserves and limits on fishing.

These observations also relate to this magnificent book created by Lawson Wood. He and I share the hope that the beautiful images and eloquent descriptions contained in the following pages will encourage others to enjoy these treasures of the Caribbean and, most importantly, to take action. The reefs need help and who can speak more eloquently on their behalf than divers, the people who intimately know their secrets and have been touched by their beauty?

Jean-Michel Cousteau

WORLD LOCATOR

HAMILTON
Bermuda
Bermuda

NORTH ATLANTIC OCEAN

Bahamas
Turks & Caicos Islands

CUBA
HAITI DOMINICAN REPUBLIC

BERMUDA LOCATOR

RTH

ATLANTIC

Samana Cay

French Cays
ug Corner *Mayaguana*
ns Island
Abraham's Bay

Little Inagua
North Caicos
Providenciales *Grand Caicos*
West Caicos *East Caicos*
Caicos Islands *South Caicos*
French Cays *Grand Turk Island*
reat Inagua
Ambergris Cays *Salt Cay*
Seal Cays *Turks Islands*
atthew
own
Southeast Point

OCEAN

Île de la Tortue
ort-de-Paix **Puerto Plata**

Santiago

Puerto Rico Trench *Leeward Islands*

de la Gonàve **HAITI**
Île de la Gonàve **DOMINICAN REPUBLIC**
Anegada
Port-Au-Prince
Tortola
Arecibo **San Juan** *St Thomas* *Virgin Gorda* *Sombrero*
Culebra *Anguilla*
El Macao **Fajardo** *St John* *Dog Island* *St Martin*
Cayes **Jacmel** **Mayagüez** **PUERTO RICO** *Virgin Islands* *Anegada Passage* *St Barthélemy*
Île-à-Vache *Mona* **Ponce** *Vieques*
Santo
Barahona **Domingo** *Cabo Rojo* *St Croix* *Saba* *St Eustatius* **Codrington**
Cabo Falso *Isla Saona* **Frederiksted** **Christiansted** *St Kitts* *Barbuda*
Isla Beata **Basseterre** **St John's**
Cabo Beata **Charlestown** *Nevis* *Antigua*
Redonda
Plymouth *Montserrat*

A
n
t *i* *l* *l* *e* *s*

Guadeloupe *La Désirade*
Basse Terre **Pointe-à-Pitre**
Iles des Saintes *Marie Galante*

Portsmouth
Roseau *Dominica*

Windward Islands
Lesser Antilles
Sainte Marie
Martinique
Fort-de-France

SEA

Castries
St Lucia
Vieux Fort

Georgetown **Speightstown**
Barbado
Kingstown *St Vincent*
Bequia **Bridgetown**
Mustique
Canouan
Union
Carriacou
Ronde
St George's *Grenada*

Dutch Antilles

Punta Gallinas *Aruba*
Oranjestad
Noord Punt *Bonaire*
Punta *Cabo San Román* **Curaçao** *Islas Los* *Cayo* *Isla La*
Espada **Willemstad** *Aves* *Roques* *Grande* *Orchila* *Isla La*
Peninsula de **Kralendijk** *Islas Las* *Cayo de Sal* *Blanquilla* *Tobago* **Charlotteville**
Peninsula de *Guajira* *Aves* *Los Testigos* **Canaan**
Paraguaná
Ríohacha **Punto Fijo** *Galera Point*
Isla de Margarita
Coro **Juangriego** *Los Testigos* **Port of Spain**
Isla La **Porlamar** *Trinidad*
Tortuga *Isla Cubagua* *Isla Coche* **San Fernando**
COLOMBIA **Maiquetía** **Carúpano** **Bonasse**
VENEZUELA **Caracas** *Galeota Point*
lledupar **Maracaibo** **Cumaná**
Puerto Cabello **Los Teques**

The name Caribbean was originally coined by the Europeans after the indigenous Carib Indians who first explored and settled amidst this vast archipelago. Covering 2,718,200km² (1,049,500 square miles), the Caribbean Sea is bordered to the west by the central American countries of Mexico, Belize, Guatemala, Nicaragua, Costa Rica, Panama and Honduras, to the south by Colombia and Venezuela, to the east

In the western Caribbean, true coral atolls have formed as mountains have submerged, creating a ring of pearl-like sand cays and tiny scrubby islands, of which Arrecife Chinchorro is the largest coral atoll in the northern hemisphere. Similar large atolls are also to be found off the coast of Belize (these are Lighthouse Reef, Glover Reef and Turneffe Island) and off the northern coast of Venezuela.

This vast sea is home to a great variety of marine life, including hundreds of species of fish, colourful sponges, invertebrates and corals, many of which are found nowhere else in the world. In the eastern regions there is a curious mix of animals also associated with the western Atlantic, and large pelagic animals ride in on these nutrient-rich waters; they include tuna, manta rays, eagle rays, and the largest fish in the sea, the whale shark.

by the crescent island chain of the Windward and Leeward islands, known collectively as the Lesser Antilles, and to the north by Cuba, Jamaica, Haiti/Dominican Republic and Puerto Rico. The latter are the largest of all the Caribbean islands and also the geographical northern limit of the Caribbean Sea; to the north of Cuba lies the vast expanse of water known as the Gulf of Mexico.

The Caribbean and her attendant land masses were formed during the last ice age, geologically speaking not so long ago. Much of this subtropical continent was hundreds of metres above sea level at that time, and caves with stalagmites and stalactites, now underwater, can be found in every corner of the Caribbean. Similarities in undersea topography and geology are found throughout the region, particularly in the simultaneous formation of the blue holes in the Bahamas and the cenotes in Mexico – testimony to the fact that all these underwater caverns were once on dry land.

The barrier reef found off the coast of Belize and Mexico is the second largest in the world, and the reef that extends from northern Cuba to the British Virgin Island of Anegada is known to be the second-largest barrier reef in the Caribbean and the third largest in the world.

GOLDEN RULES

Divers often inadvertently damage coral reefs. Listed below are a few points to keep in mind when diving off the Caribbean coral reefs.

- Avoid touching coral with your hands, fins, tanks, etcetera
- Do not wear gloves
- Never stand on coral
- Do not collect any marine life
- Avoid overweighting and work on your buoyancy control (see panel, right)
- Do not feed the fish alien foods as this could be harmful to them
- Make sure your equipment consoles do not drag on the coral
- Do not use spear guns
- Do not molest marine life, in particular turtles, pufferfish and sea urchins
- Do not climb inside barrel sponges
- Through your interactions, consider your impact on aquatic life
- Report environmental disturbances or destruction of any dive sites

Humpback whales are known to migrate up the Antilles and can be found from November to February around the Silver Banks near the Turks and Caicos Islands. Sperm whales cross the Atlantic from the Azores to the northeast and are often seen off the east coast of Dominica. Many of the islands have indigenous populations of dolphins and manatees. Dolphins are also found in several sanctuaries, where they regularly interact with divers and snorkellers. One of the most famous dolphin experiences in the area is with UNEXSO (see page 136) at Freeport in the Bahamas; other similar encounters can be enjoyed in Roatan in the Bay Islands of Honduras, and there is also a wild, but habituated dolphin called JoJo in Providenciales in the Turks and Caicos Islands. Pods of wild dolphins can be encountered in several areas, including Panama City in Florida, Honduras and Curaçao.

Above from left to right The orange ball corallimorph *(Pseudocorynactis caribbeorum)*, the giant anemone *(Condylactis gigantea)*, branching tube sponges *(Pseudoceratina crassa)*, and the flamingo tongue mollusc *(Cyphoma gibbosum)*.

Many people have been known to associate tropical waters with sharks and, although they are generally quite rare in this region, the most common are the Caribbean reef shark and the nurse shark. Again, several diver interaction dives have been organized in the Bahamas over a number of years and nowadays there are many different locations where divers can experience the thrill of their lives.

Blackbeard and Henry Morgan. Many ships foundered on the dangerous low-lying reefs and sand bars which form a virtually impenetrable barrier in the eastern Caribbean; these and the periodic hurricanes wreaked havoc on the ships. One of the most famous of all the Caribbean wrecks is that of the Royal Mail Steamer *Rhone* which foundered in the British Virgin Islands in 1875.

The islands are all situated in the hurricane belt, with the rainy season starting around the beginning of June and lasting for six months – but do not let this deter you from visiting the islands during the rest of the year, as the months of April and May are deemed the quiet season, and also present some of the best diving.

The Windward Islands have some excellent dives. Grenada is known for the wreck of the

Much of what we see in the Caribbean is only in the upper surface waters. However, the coral organisms form a thin, delicate, living film on the ancient bony skeletons of their ancestors, and it is amongst these tropical reefs that scuba divers venture. There are a number of locations where 'wall diving' is the norm, where the fringing island reef or barrier reef plunges for 2000m (6600 ft) or more. Scuba divers mostly explore around the shallow fringing reefs which all the Caribbean islands have in great abundance.

The Caribbean Sea was well known as the commercial seaway of the treasure-laden Spanish and French fleets which plied the trade routes amongst these treacherous reefs and islands, carrying their ill-gotten gains back to Europe. Not all this treasure managed to cross the Caribbean en route to the Atlantic and home; much of it fell prey to pirates such as the infamous

Above from left to right The sculptured slipper lobster *(Parribachus antarcticus)*, the lovely queen angelfish *(Holacanthus ciliaris)*, a balloonfish *(Diodon holacanthus)* resting among sponges, and a pair of rainbow parrotfish *(Scarus guacamaia)*.

BUOYANCY CONTROL

As an underwater photographer, I am constantly aware of contact sometimes made with the coral reef. It is essential that all divers master the art of buoyancy control. The idea is to be able to hover horizontally and vertically close to the reef or the bottom without touching either. Buoyancy is controlled by inflating or deflating the buoyancy compensator at various depths. Once expert buoyancy has been achieved there will be a drastic reduction on your air consumption; you will see more marine life on each dive; you will dramatically cut down on accidental environmental damage and your pleasure will increase proportionately.

Photographers who use extension tubes with attached framers on the lens will have to touch the reef in order to take the photograph. If you do have to touch the reef, use only one finger for leverage to hold you still or to push you off, and then only on dead coral.

Bianca C, a cruise ship that sank on 24 October 1961. Now upright in 50m (165ft) of water, this wreck is a dive for very experienced divers only, as there are generally strong surface currents here. In Dominica, most diving is done between Scott's Head and Roseau where several coral pinnacles, particularly Soufriere Pinnacle and Scott's Head Pinnacle, come very close to the surface and are favoured by both divers and snorkellers.

Martinique and Guadeloupe are part of the French Antilles, which also include St Martin and St Barthélemy in the Leeward Islands. Martinique's Pointe Burgos, located between Pointe Lezarde and Rocher du Diamant (Diamond Rock), is known for its large resident school of Atlantic spadefish. Diamond Rock off the southwest coast is a spectacular site of vertical walls, gullies, canyons and caves, covered in gorgonian sea fans; there is an above average chance of coming across large pelagics here.

Off the southern coast of Basse Terre in Guadeloupe is the Cousteau Marine Reserve, with a lovely coral garden around the small island of Petit Ilet, also known as Jacks Reef. Nearby, off Grand Ilet, is a series of hot water springs, testimony to the island's volcanic origins.

St Vincent's New Guinea Reef is a popular wall dive starting at around 12m (40ft). The Gardens near the capital of Kingston are known for frogfish and sea horses. In Bequia (pronounced 'Beckway'), L'Anse Chemin is a very popular drift dive known for its large numbers of flamingo tongue shells; it is 30 minutes by boat from Admiralty Bay. Horseshoe Reef in the Tobago Cays is a spectacular reef circling four of the islands and is popular with snorkellers and divers alike.

Barbados is more isolated than the other islands and sits squarely in the Atlantic, about 500km (300 miles) northeast of Venezuela. Dottlin's Reef, situated along the sheltered west coast, is perhaps the prettiest reef in Barbados. Depths start at around 20m (66ft), and the marine life is superb.

Some of the riches you may encounter in the Caribbean are the curious arrow crab, the spotted drumfish, or the splendid toadfish, indigenous to Mexico and Cozumel, which hides in a coral cave and uses the cavern as an amplifier for it to 'croak' and attract its mate. Tiny blennies, wrasse and gobies, as well as a number of shrimps, act as 'cleaners' to many other marine organisms. Everywhere in the Caribbean you are able to see predators and prey lining up at these cleaning stations, all enmity forgotten, to be 'cleaned' of parasites and dead or decaying scales or flesh. Colourful anemones stretch out their stinging tentacles to catch unwary prey, and coral sea fans sway

gracefully in the current. Delicate angelfish swim around these corals and sponges. In the Cayman Islands, one of the true marvels of the underwater world can be found – in just one metre of water, tourists can mingle freely with an ever growing family of over 250 stingrays. They are the southern stingrays *(Dasyatis americana)* which have become habituated to human presence and free hand-outs of food. When the feeding frenzy passes, the creatures very quickly revert to their normal feeding habit of searching the sand flats for molluscs, crabs and worms.

From Cuba to Venezuela, from Honduras to Barbados, the sport of scuba diving is very professionally organized and generally comes under the auspices of PADI (the Professional Association of Diving Instructors). All divers must be properly certified by a responsible agency and have a minimum qualification or 'C' card. Those wishing to penetrate shipwrecks, caves and caverns, dive deeper into any of the many blue holes, or even dive at night, must obtain special training from qualified instructors; this will greatly enhance their enjoyment and make provision for as great a safety margin as possible.

In a book such as *Top Dive Sites of the Caribbean,* it would be unrealistic to compare one location with another; each island or coral reef has its own individually splendid dives. The Bahamas are known for their sharks and shallow coral reefs; Bonaire and Curaçao are renowned for the tiny animals that provide really wonderful opportunities for macrophotography; Cozumel is probably the top site in the Caribbean for drift diving. However, there are many lesser known reefs and atolls that also yield some truly special dives, whether you dive on wrecks amidst thousands of silverside minnows, or

CLASSIFICATION AND NOMENCLATURE

The scientific name or nomenclature of a particular animal is very important. When diving in various parts of the world, or even in the same region, you may come across several different names for the same creature. This can be confusing. When identifying or describing a particular animal, scientists prefer to use its scientific or specific name.

The correct naming of a species is very important for your own log book records and is essential to scientists and marine biologists studying the flora and fauna both now and in the future. The modern binominal system of nomenclature was developed by Linnaeus and dates from the publication of his *Systema Naturae* in 1758 and subsequent years.

The Latin name of the animal contains the name of the genus to which it belongs, which always has a capital letter; this is followed by the specific or trivial name which is always spelt with a small letter, i.e. *Mycteroperca tigris* (tiger grouper). Once you start using scientific names, you soon find how easy it is and how good for describing species to other enthusiasts in a common language.

just enjoy yourself floating around in the shallows. The choice of islands and dive sites featured here is purely subjective, but gleaned from many hundreds of hours spent exploring the spectacular underwater world of the Caribbean.

Opposite The banded coral shrimp *(Stenopus hispidus)* is the largest of the Caribbean cleaner shrimps.

Left The red night shrimp *(Rhinchocinetes rigens)* hides during the day and is only seen at night.

Following pages The cleaning goby perches on brain corals, waiting for a meal.

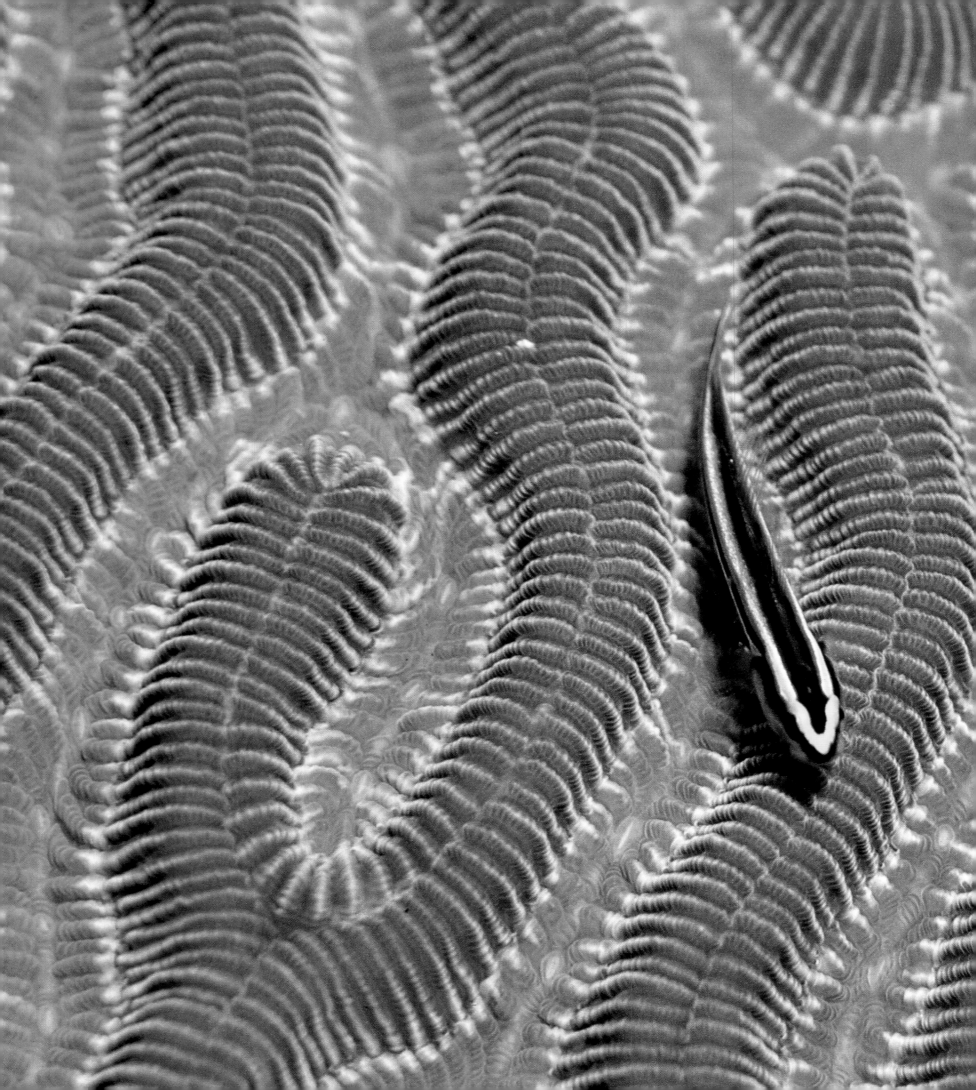

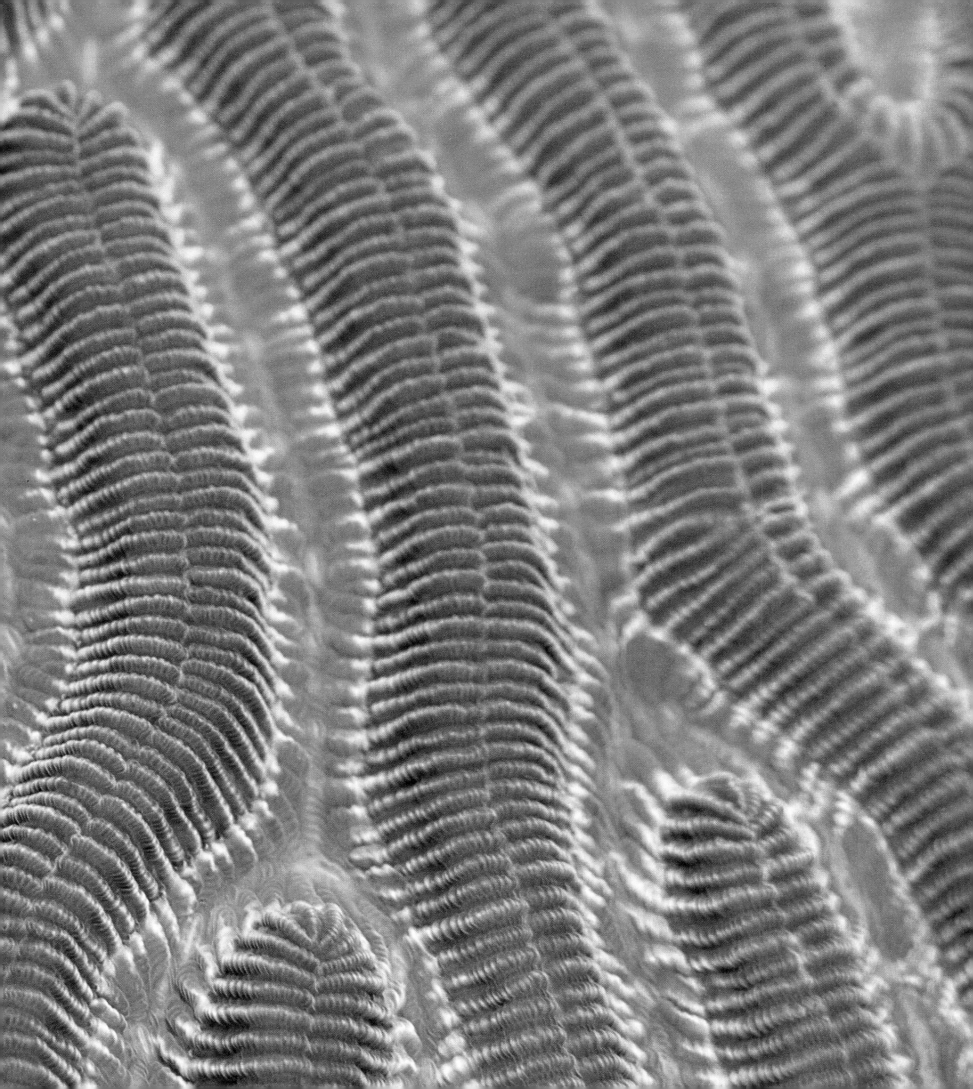

GREATER ANTILLES

Known for having some of the clearest water and greatest diversity of marine life in the Caribbean, the Greater Antilles is not only the largest group of islands in the region but also covers the greatest part of the Caribbean Sea. Bordered by the Gulf of Mexico to the north and the Caribbean Sea to the south, the Greater Antilles comprise the islands of Puerto Rico, Haiti/Dominican Republic (previously known as Hispaniola) and Cuba, as well as Jamaica and the Cayman Islands, both of which lie entirely in the Caribbean. Off the northern coast of Cuba, and stretching west to the Virgin Islands and Anegada, is the second-largest barrier reef in the Caribbean – and the third largest in the world. The deepest part of the Caribbean Sea is the Cayman Trench at 7658m (25,126ft).

PUERTO RICO

New Diving in an Old Country

ANGEL REEF · CAYO RATON · CAYO LOBOS · THE CRACKS · BLACK WALL · DESECHEO

*P*uerto Rico has been under US sovereignty since 1893 and has a population of around four million people. Located approximately 1600km (1000 miles) south of Miami, this semitropical island has approximately 432km (270 miles) of coastline and encompasses lovely palm-fringed beaches, a lush tropical rainforest and, in the southwestern region, a dry desertlike habitat with rolling hills inhabited by thousands and thousands of birds.

The island is dominated by a range of mountains known as the Cordillera Centrál, the massive peaks of which extend to a height of about 1338m (4390ft). Fabulous waterfalls cascade down the slopes of the Cordillera Centrál and then make their way to the sea. In the north, near the town of Arecibo, the waters fall into spectacular caves and sink holes. The Camuy River, for example, disappears into a blue hole near Lares and a number of the caves in the karst limestone region can even be explored by tram.

San Juan, the capital city of Puerto Rico, features two completely different and distinct neighbourhoods. The Old Town is an interesting area to explore and is dominated by the ancient 16th-century fort of El Morro, which stands on a promontory situated some 42m (140ft) above the crashing waves. The newer part of San Juan, also known as 'Little Miami', is quite close to the airport, which has become the central hub for the majority of Caribbean air traffic. San Juan is characterized by crowded architecture in the Spanish style, and also boasts some really superb antique shops.

Not far from San Juan is El Yunque, the only tropical rainforest in the US Forest Service, with its many magnificent hiking trails and spectacular driving routes. The scenic highway that goes from Tuna Point (or Manaubo) to Mayagüez is particularly beautiful. The hills around Guanica are lavishly decked in the world's largest dry coastal forest, which has now been designated an international biosphere reserve.

Diving in the region is concentrated along Puerto Rico's east and west coasts, principally on the small offshore islands and surrounding reefs, where the average depth of the dive sites is approximately 20m (66ft). To the east of Puerto Rico lie the beautiful islands of Vieques and Culebra – part of a small chain of islands situated midway between Puerto Rico and St Thomas of the United States Virgin Islands – islands that geographically form the northern limit of the Caribbean Sea. Vieques can be reached in about 20 minutes by small aeroplane from Fajardo or San Juan on the mainland, or alternatively by means of an hour-long passenger ferry trip from Fajardo, which costs a mere US$2. The same ferry can be taken from the mainland to Culebra, and at the same price.

Best time to go In May–Sept the weather is most settled and the sea is calm. The best underwater visibility is from Nov–Mar.

Climate Easterly trade winds keep the air and water temperature at an average 28°C (82°F). Water temperature drops by 7°F from Nov–May; full wetsuits are advisable.

Getting there San Juan is considered to be the major airport in the Caribbean; virtually every airline has links to Puerto Rico. Mayagüez and Aguadilla have airports that are serviced by regular, daily internal flights.

Special interest Mona and Desecheo, west of Puerto Rico, are known for sightings of dolphins and humpback whales in Jan.

Accommodation and dive operations In La Parguera, stay in one of two state-owned *paradores*, or small hotels: Parador Posada Porlamar and Parador Villa Parguera. Copamarina Beach Resort is a beachfront dive resort in Guanica. San Juan has all the major hotel chains, costing around US$100 per night. Caribe Aquatic Services (at the Radisson Normandie) and the Caribbean School of Aquatics offer dives from San Juan. Culebra Dive Resort has accommodation. On the west coast, stay in Joyuda and dive with Aquatica Underwater Adventures or South West Scuba.

Electricity supply American-style plugs, 110–120V at 60 cycles.

Emergency information The closest recompression chamber is on St Thomas, US Virgin Islands. Tel: (340) 776 2686.

Previous pages The south side of Little Cayman Island with the islet of Owen Island in the foreground.
Opposite The queen angelfish *(Holacanthus ciliaris)* is the most colourful of all the Caribbean angelfish.
Top Foureye butterflyfish *(Chaetodon capistratus)* have an eye marking near the tail to confuse predators.

Angel Reef

Some 20 minutes by boat to the southwest of Esperanza, a town situated on the island of Vieques, Angel Reef is located with the assistance of a handheld Global Positioning System (GPS). Lying approximately 1.5km (1 mile) offshore, the reef comprises a classic spur-and-groove formation that runs perpendicular to the shore. The top of the reef is only 12m (40ft) below the surface of the water and is smothered in sea fans, rods and plumes. Well known for its numerous angelfish, particularly the grey angelfish (*Pomacanthus arcuatus*), the reef's other attraction is a pair of ancient Spanish anchors – one lying on top of the reef, and the other one deeply embedded at the bottom of the reef at about 18m (60ft). Offshore reefs generally tend to be a bit choppy on the surface, and Angel Reef is no exception. There is, however, no ground swell underwater and also very little current, making it a comfortable dive. At the bottom of the reef the corals give way to a wide sand chute that slopes off into deeper water. Here you will find garden eels (*Heteroconger halis*), as well as sand tile fish (*Malacanthus plumieri*) which build their nests in the sand out of coral rubble.

Cayo Raton

Cayo Raton, otherwise known as Rat Key, is one of the larger uninhabited islets located to the southwest of the island of Culebra. The dive boat at this site is anchored in a small cove situated to the north of the rock, from where a submarine plateau extends and drops down to approximately 15m (50ft). This is a superb shallow dive, made all the more exciting by the numerous species of schooling fish that move as one across the shallow reefs at around 6–9m (20–30ft).

Although lacking in decent-sized hard corals, Cayo Raton has numerous sea fans, whips and rods. It also has queen angelfish (*Holacanthus ciliaris*), spotfin butterflyfish (*Chaetodon ocellatus*) and banded butterflyfish (*Chaetodon striatus*). Creole wrasse (*Clepticus parrai*) are common here, swimming along the top of the reef where they mingle with blue chromis (*Chromis cyanea*). One of the most colourful of the Caribbean moray eels, the chain moray (*Echidna catenata*), is found here. Usually shy during the day, it hides under coral ledges and rocky overhangs, only venturing out at night to feed amongst the corals, searching for sleeping fish and unwary crustaceans.

Above Queen angelfish (*Holacanthus ciliaris*) are generally solitary fish and are rarely seen in pairs.

Above A pair of grey angelfish (*Pomacanthus arcuatus*) roam the reefs near San Juan; they are by far the friendliest of the angelfish species.

Left The chain moray eel (*Echidna catenata*), with its short blunt teeth, hides under coral rubble during the day and feeds at night, primarily on crustaceans.

Cayo Lobos

This small offshore island northeast of Puerto Rico is generally reached by boat from Fajardo or San Juan. It has an excellent fringing reef that drops from quite close to the surface to approximately 9m (30ft) and is made up of many different varieties of coral, including large cactus coral (*Mycetophyllia lamarckiana*), lettuce coral (*Agaricia agaricites*) and sheet coral (*Agaricia lamarcki*). Giant sea rods (*Plexaurella nutans*), swaying in the current, are home to flamingo tongue shells (*Cyphoma gibbosum*). These molluscs have a brightly coloured mantle, or outer skin, that is covered in flamboyant spots. The small islands in the vicinity of Puerto Rico are also known for regular sightings of manatees. When the water temperature rises during summer, these gentle creatures swim out to the outer reefs. At other times they reside in the mangrove and grassy lagoons associated with the mainland.

CLEANING STATIONS

Cleaning stations are areas of the coral reef and sandy sea bed where a host of small creatures perform a vital function in the ecology of a thriving ecosystem – they clean parasites and decaying food matter from reef fishes and remove dead skin or scales from wounds.

The cleaners you are most likely to see are gobies of the genus *Gobiosoma*. Several species of this tiny fish set up 'shop' on hard corals such as brain coral and boulder star coral; they are rarely found elsewhere, except on a few of the larger sponges. Cleaning gobies are characterized by striped bodies and a V-shaped design on their heads. Flitting about in short bursts of speed, they wait for fish to enter the 'safe zone' and indicate their wish to be cleaned. Large fish such as snapper or grouper signal this intent by opening their gill covers and mouths, allowing the little fish to swim through. Once the session is over, the larger fish will close their mouths gently, thus allowing the cleaners time to swim free.

Above *Periclimenes yucatanicus* is a colourful cleaner shrimp. It has a symbiotic relationship with its host anemone, *Condylactis gigantea*.

Juvenile bluehead wrasse and hogfish also act as cleaners. Whereas gobies have a fairly fixed station, wrasse and hogfish are more opportunistic cleaners. Juvenile female bluehead wrasse *(Thalassoma bifasciatum)* have streamlined yellow bodies and a dark spot on the dorsal fin. They often feed around anemones. Juvenile Spanish hogfish *(Bodianus rufus)* have purple coloration on the head, changing to gold mid-body; only very young juveniles will act as cleaners. When wrasse and hogfish are ready to clean, they dart into the water column and challenge other fish into a submissive posture; the fish wanting to be cleaned will open their mouths. Once this action starts, more fish line up, especially jacks, and this in turn attracts even more cleaners.

Pederson's cleaning shrimp *(Periclimenes pedersoni)*, once thought to be the major cleaning shrimp in the Caribbean, actually only performs its cleaning function as a ruse to get its main source of food – the protective mucus coating which covers all fish. Occurring at the entrances to small holes in the reef or under boulders on the sea bed, where corkscrew anemones *(Bartholomea annulata)* are common, they attract attention by waving and flicking their white antennae.

The very colourful spotted cleaner shrimp *(Periclimenes yucatanicus)* is always seen in association with the giant anemone *(Condylactis gigantea)* and the elegant anemone *(Actinoporus elegans)*. These are the most common shrimps in Curaçao, particularly around the *Tugboat* (*see* page 74). The squat anemone shrimp *(Thor amboinensis)* is also found on these two anemones – they clean as much as small blennies and gobies.

The scarlet-striped cleaning shrimp *(Lysmata grabhami)* is often seen around the head, mouth and gills of many species of large grouper, and the peppermint shrimp *(L. wurdemanni)* sets up shop in large pink vase sponges. The banded coral shrimp *(Stenopus hispidus)*, which hides under overhangs and in crevices, waving its white antennae to attract attention, occurs in all of the world's tropical oceans.

The very nature of the cleaning function creates 'safe zones' all over the reefs where predators and prey can be seen waiting alongside each other as this social truce is enforced. These cleaning creatures are not just individuals struggling to survive – they are part of an incredibly complex integrated structure that works according to a firm set of guidelines which they must all follow to keep them fit and healthy.

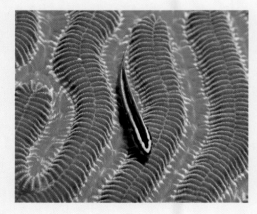

Above The cleaning goby *(Gobiosoma genie)* is the most common of all the cleaner fish and is found on hard corals all over the Caribbean.

Above Here a grouper opens its mouth wide to allow cleaners to enter safely and pick debris from its teeth and gills.

Above This particular cleaner shrimp *(Lysmata wurdemanni)* sets up 'shop' at the entrance to an azure vase sponge.

The Cracks

Just around 10 minutes by boat from the marina at Palmas Del Mar, in Puerto Rico, this inshore sea bed reef of limestone rock has been carved and eroded over the centuries to create large overhanging ledges that come together in places to form long tunnels, trenches, caves, caverns and archways. While the average depth is 15–21m (50–70ft), this dive site can be influenced by surge, although it only has the effect of making conditions on the surface more difficult. Underwater, there are large, orange elephant's ear sponges (*Agelas clathrodes*) and a brilliant yellow boring sponge (*Siphonodictyom coralliphagum*), which eats into live corals.

Black Wall

When you depart from Paraguera on the mainland, you will notice that the sheltered inner lagoon is always serene and calm as you travel towards the outer edge of the low-lying, offshore islands, where the depth of the ocean floor then suddenly drops away hundreds of metres below you. Black Wall is well known for its scooped-out bowl formation, which is fringed in delicate black corals and sea fans. Branching tube sponges (*Pseudoceratina crassa*) form in large clumps and stove-pipe sponges (*Aplysina archeri*) can be found in deeper water.

Spanish hogfish are quite common at Black Wall, as are the brilliantly coloured basslets. Both the fairy basslet (*Gramma loreto*) and the blackcap basslet (*Gramma melacara*) are very often found in fairly large numbers on the wall, frequently swimming upside down as they attempt to align themselves to the curvature of the coral caves.

Desecheo

Situated 21km (15 miles) west of the surfing community of Rincón on Puerto Rico's northwest coast, the tiny, uninhabited island of Desecheo takes about 45 minutes to reach by boat, in what is often quite choppy water. The effort, however, is worth any discomfort that may be experienced on the trip. The island is a subterranean mountain which rises from the Puerto Rican Trench – the second deepest in the Caribbean – from a depth of about 9000m (30,000ft). The overall impression is of an incredibly healthy reef, festooned in a multitude of corals and sponges and surrounded by fish. Many of the overhanging ledges are covered in orange cup corals (*Tubastrea coccinea*), which make for a dazzling experience, particularly at night when the whole of the reef seems to be bathed in a yellow glow. Large pelagic fish are also quite common here, and there are regular sightings of dolphins.

Below The lovely flamingo tongue shell *(Cyphoma gibbosum)* is perhaps the most commonly found and most colourful of all the Caribbean molluscs.

Above Orange cup corals *(Tubastrea coccinea)*, the size of your fingernail, are light sensitive, extending their polyps to feed at night.

CUBA

A Destination Waiting to be Explored

MARIA LA GORDA · ISLE OF YOUTH · CAYO LARGO

Best time to go Jun–Dec, when the prevailing wind is east-southeast.

Climate The dry season is from Nov–Apr and the wet season from May–Oct. The average air temperature is 25.6°C (78°F) and rainfall is around 1380mm (54in).

Getting there Daily international flights from a number of European cities, as well as from Mexico, Puerto Rico and South America. There are still no direct flights to Cuba from the United States.

Special interest You can spend quite a lot of time exploring this vast and diverse country. Discover its historical past, trek the nature parks or snorkel around miles and miles of empty coastline. A tour of Havana is particularly recommended, as is a visit to Trinidad.

Accommodation and dive operations The International Dive Centre, in the Villa International in Cayo Largo and in the Colony Hotel on the Isle of Youth; Puertosol Dive Centre is at the Hotel Maria La Gorda, Maria La Gorda; the *MV Boca del Toro* operates along the Jardines Bank.

Emergency information The main re-compression chamber is at the Hospital Luis Diaz Soto in Havana. Tel: 60 28 04, 68 32 41, or 68 32 66. There are a number of smaller chambers in other towns and at the Colony Hotel on the Isle of Youth. All emergencies are routed through the central switchboard and are then rerouted to the chamber closest to the emergency area.

By far the largest island in the Caribbean, the Republic of Cuba lies 145km (90 miles) southeast of Florida and is bordered by the Caribbean Sea to the south and the Gulf of Mexico to the north and west. Although only recently opened up to sport diving, Cuba is believed to have the largest diversity of marine life to be found in the entire Caribbean. Its 5746km-long (3563-mile) coastline remains largely unexplored.

Cuba has had a somewhat checkered history, having been settled originally by Arawak Indians, who were then enslaved by the Spanish.

The island was sold to Britain in 1762 and then swapped with Florida, after which it remained, for the most part, under Spanish rule until 1899 when the USA moved in. In 1952, Fulgencio Batista staged a coup d'etat and took control of Cuba. Finally in 1959, after years of discontent, Fidel Castro came into power and Cuba became the first communist republic in the western hemisphere.

With its colonial architecture and 17th-century castles and forts, Havana, the capital, is a must for all visitors. To the east of Havana is Trinidad, a town that was fully restored by funds from UNESCO and ordained a World Heritage Site. In fact, besides the southwestern side of the island, where the more favourable dive resorts are located, much of the island is unspoiled and waiting to be explored.

The most popular sites include Maria La Gorda (meaning 'Maria, the fat one'), situated at the western tip of Cuba; the Isle of Youth (Isla de La Juventud), which lies 100km (62 miles) south of the mainland; and Cayo Largo, situated to the east of the Isle of Youth. Although diving is one of the most rapidly expanding sports in Cuba, it is still concentrated only in small, very localized areas – with the exception of the few live-aboard dive boats that are now exploring further afield.

Cuba is essentially off limits to American citizens, except for those who enter via the Mexican back door, and, instead, it is the most rapidly expanding destination in the Caribbean for Canadians, Mexicans and Europeans. European money is being invested in the tourism industry, with many fine resorts being built all over the island. Despite the rapid development, diving in Cuba is still in its infancy and, if you want to experience what the Caribbean's marine life was like 20 years ago, this is the place for you.

With the end of the Cold War, many former military ships are now being sold off and sunk in prime positions all around the Caribbean as part of a massive artificial reef programme, and as additional diver attractions. These ships very quickly become part of the underwater world, first of all being colonized by algae, then by corals and all of their attendant fish and invertebrates.

Opposite The Isle of Youth is very popular with divers as it offers deep-water diving close to the shore.
Top Underwater caverns are a great attraction to divers, considerably heightening the dive experience.

dive centre and renowned for its vertical drop-off and a shaft which drops through the outer reef. Access is through a narrow cave entrance at 14m (47ft), which funnels down immediately so that there is space for only one diver to enter at a time. It is quite exhilarating, although only for advanced divers. The wall is covered in sponges, hanging corals and algae – and hermit crabs, shrimps, blennies and gobies are everywhere. The reef top is alive with creole wrasse and blue chromis.

Isle Of Youth

The barrier reef that runs along Cuba's south coast has created a large number of small cays and islands, many miles offshore, comprising the Jardines Bank, Cayo Blanco and the Isle of Youth. The reef wall comes very close to the shore around the Isle of Youth and it is this aspect, plus the depth of the vertical underwater walls, that has brought divers back year after year.

Again, most dive sites in the region are marked by numbered mooring buoys from which the sites derive their names. Dive number 22, for example,

Above The Isle of Youth has sheer walls that come very close to the shore, making it a popular area.

Maria La Gorda

Diving at Maria La Gorda is accessible all year round due to the sheltered nature of the wide bay. The 30 or so dive sites, marked by mooring buoys, run in a north–south direction with the wall starting close to the shore at around 14m (47ft), before plummeting beyond safe diving depths. Most of the wall diving is accomplished by swimming over the lip edge, or by entering one of the many caves or passageways that wind through the reef crest, and exiting onto the outside of the wall at around 30m (100ft). These dives are in fact very similar to Bloody Bay Wall in the Cayman Islands.

A fine example is Encanto I with its huge coral buttresses, many of which are connected, creating caves. Other coral buttresses come so close together that they have formed tunnels and canyons that wind through the reef. Where sunlight cuts through the reef, it creates impressive, illuminated shafts. The site is characterized by huge barrel sponges, rope sponges, gorgonian sea fans and regular large groups of barracuda that hover over you. Larger pelagics and big grouper might be lacking, but the reef structure and marine life more than make up for this.

Another marked site is Yemaya, a headland located less than a 10-minute boat ride from the

UNUSUAL INHABITANTS OF THE CARIBBEAN

Below A juvenile spotted drum 'dances' near a coral cave; this creature only becomes spotted when it reaches adulthood.

Often difficult to spot because it is very small and only performs at night, the juvenile spotted drum (*Equetus punctatus*) is well worth searching for. As a juvenile, it has three broad, vertical, black stripes down its white body, the largest stripe continuing from the tip of its elongated dorsal fin to the end of its long tail. These fish become more 'fish-shaped' and spotted only when they reach adulthood. Their curious dance is an absolute delight to observe.

One of the fish that frequently appeared in Greek mythology was the sea horse. In the Caribbean, the most commonly seen member of the species is the longsnout sea horse (*Hippocampus reidi*). These are quite plentiful

along the shores of Bonaire (*see* page 65) at Captain Don's Habitat and under the Town Pier. Their natural capability of staying still and their ability to change colour like a chameleon makes it very hard to find them, unless they are of a strongly contrasting colour because of having just moved from one location to the next.

Above Longsnout sea horses (*Hippocampus reidi*) are like underwater chameleons, changing colour to blend in with their surroundings.

might not sound very attractive, but is very practical from the point of view of the dive shops.

The wall starts at 20m (66ft) and drops vertically off the continental shelf. Everywhere you look there are huge sponges, many of which overhang the wall along with sheet corals and algae.

Several sites have huge caverns, tunnels and canyons that wind down through the wall, where shade-loving creatures and fish congregate in large numbers. Tarpon (*Megalops atlanticus*) are in abundance, rounding up shoals of silversides – a collective name for the young of four different fish families that gather together for protection. Snapper and grunt are common, as are numerous species of parrotfish, particularly stoplight parrotfish (*Sparisoma viride*) and princess parrotfish (*Scarus taeniopterus*).

Shipwrecks in Siguanea Cove, north of Cape Francés, offer

very interesting dives, particularly the *Jibacoa River*, *Sparta* and *New Grove*, which were sunk approximately 20 years ago and used by the military for target practice. These coral- and sponge-encrusted superstructures are almost an extension of the Cuban coral reef system, and attract a multitude of fish.

Cayo Largo

One of the larger, most easterly islands is Cayo Largo, east of the Isle of Youth in the Archipelago de los Canarreos on the outer edge of the Jardines de la Reina Bank. Much of the diving here takes place from the marina at Puerto Sol, and there are over 30 sites marked by mooring buoys to prevent anchor damage to any part of the barrier reef.

The outer edge of this barrier reef drops vertically in many places, cut by immense sand chutes where garden eels (*Heteroconger halis*) stretch out into the current as they feed on plankton. Arrow crabs (*Stenorhynchus seticornis*) are found in profusion,

as well as the flamingo tongue (*Cyphoma gibbosum*), a common mollusc shell found only in the Caribbean. Along the edge of the sand chutes coral growth is profuse. Massive barrel sponges, tube sponges and virtually every species of hard and soft coral that are resident in the area are represented on these thriving slopes.

Further excellent diving is found along Los Jardines de la Reina to the east of Cayo Largo. For divers, the attraction of this area of the Jardines Bank is that you see very few other divers here, as much of the terrain is unexplored. A new live-aboard dive boat, the *MV Boca del Toro*, is now charting this virgin territory and some fantastic dive spots have already been discovered, with regular sightings of whale sharks, eagle rays and Caribbean reef sharks. Spotted moray eels (*Gymnothorax moringa*) are the most common on the reef, while the sharptail snake eel (*Myrichthys breviceps*), normally a night hunter, can be seen regularly during the day. Queen angelfish are common, as are several different species of butterflyfish, grunt, snapper and crustaceans.

Above Sharptail snake eels (*Myrichthys breviceps*) are most commonly seen at night.

Above Arrow crabs (*Stenorhynchus seticornis*) have very long, delicate legs and pincers.

Right Balloonfish inflate themselves when danger threatens by sucking in great quantities of water which extends their defensive spines.

The creature that is the most synonymous with the Caribbean Sea is the arrow crab (*Stenorhynchus seticornis*). Pugnacious by nature, it perches at the entrance to small holes where anemones live. Covered in dark bands, it is roughly triangular in shape, with a long, tapering, pointed head and slender spider-like legs. Arrow crabs, with their unique appearance, are probably by far the most photographed of all the Caribbean crustaceans.

The balloonfish or globefish (*Diodon holocanthus*) is a species of pufferfish with long spines on its head and body, and dusky bands of colour. When threatened, it will

rapidly suck in large amounts of water until it is the size of a football. When this takes place, the spines across the body are extended and point outwards. This action renders the fish incapable of escape, but also makes it look so threatening that it is generally left well alone.

Other unusual inhabitants of the Caribbean include longlure frogfish (*Antennarius multiocellatus*), which move about over the reef with their specially adapted pectoral fins acting as 'feet', and flounders, which have adapted by becoming flat in shape and having eyes that face upwards, allowing them to exist in the flat world of their sandy-bottom habitat.

CAYMAN ISLANDS

Stingrays, Wall Diving and Wrecks

STINGRAY CITY AND THE SANDBAR • BLOODY BAY WALL • GREENHOUSE REEF

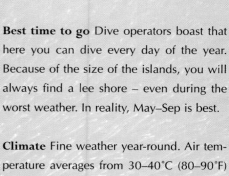

First discovered in 1503 by Christopher Columbus, the Cayman Islands are situated in the central Caribbean, south of Cuba and 290km (175 miles) northwest of Jamaica. The three coral islands, namely Grand Cayman, Cayman Brac and Little Cayman, although very American in most respects, are British crown colonies and subject to British laws and customs. Each island has its own atmosphere and, of course, offers great diving.

Grand Cayman, the largest island, is 35km (22 miles) long and world famous for Stingray City where over 250 stingrays are fed daily by tourists in waters as shallow as 1m (3ft). The north wall is legendary and there are some photogenic wrecks, one of which, the *Kirk Pride*, can only be reached by a deep submersible as it rests at 242m (800ft).

Little Cayman, the smallest of the three islands, is located 120km (75 miles) north of Grand Cayman. Its star site, Bloody Bay Wall, has been described as the best wall diving in the Caribbean. Some 11km (7 miles) away is Cayman Brac, home to a sunken Russian destroyer, which sits amid some of the best coral reefs in the region.

The Caribbean's deepest oceanic valley, the Cayman Trench, comes close to the shores of these islands and is responsible for the above-average clarity of the water and also contributes to the spectacular wall diving. The sides of the oceanic trench can be explored further in a submersible, which can travel to depths well beyond the limits of sport diving.

Besides diving, snorkelling and safe swimming, visitors to these magical islands can hire jet skis and pedaloes, take a glass-bottomed boat trip, or go parasailing or water-skiing. Shopping rounds off the list of attractions in this relaxed environment, where the locals are always welcoming.

Local dive operators are very safety-conscious and the Cayman Islands Watersports Operators Association is very proud of its safety record. The Department of the Environment, responsible for maintaining the marine parks, has introduced over 200 permanent mooring buoys around the islands. These single-pin moorings are changed annually to allow coral regeneration and to spread the load of diver pollution. The same department was also responsible for the survey and clean-up work done on the former Russian destroyer, number 356, which was sunk off Greenhouse Reef north of Cayman Brac. This hulk, now renamed the *MV Captain Keith Tibbetts*, is already home to a myriad fish and is the only divable Russian warship in the western hemisphere.

Most diving and snorkelling in the Caymans is from day boats, and usually entails a 10-minute ride to your location. You can, however, hire equipment from a number of dive centres and shore dive to your heart's content. The only live-aboard dive boat is the *Cayman Aggressor III*.

Opposite A diver emerges from a mass of silverside minnows off Bloody Bay Wall, Little Cayman Island.
Top Taking two passengers only, the *Atlantis* submersible explores the edges of the Cayman Trench.

Best time to go Dive operators boast that here you can dive every day of the year. Because of the size of the islands, you will always find a lee shore – even during the worst weather. In reality, May–Sep is best.

Climate Fine weather year-round. Air temperature averages from 30–40°C (80–90°F) in summer, dropping to a low of 20°C (70°F) during the short winter season.

Getting there Cayman Airways and 10 other scheduled air carriers fly into Grand Cayman. Depending on the time of year, Cayman Airways flies three or four times daily from Miami. It also offers daily connections between the three Cayman islands. For European travellers, British Airways, operated by Caledonian, offer a direct flight to Grand Cayman from Gatwick, London.

Special interest *Atlantis* Submersible to 240m (800ft) to the wreck of *Kirk Pride*.

Accommodation and dive operations The superb *Cayman Aggressor III* offers unlimited diving from Georgetown, Grand Cayman. For the North Wall, one of the best operations is Indies Divers (based at Indies Suites, which is self-catering). The Brac Reef Beach Resort, Cayman Brac, and the Little Cayman Beach Resort, Little Cayman, both have dive centres.

Emergency information There is a re-compression chamber on Grand Cayman, British West Indies. Tel: 1 345 949 2989 (emergency: 555). Address: PO Box 1551G, Georgetown, Grand Cayman.

Left Local snorkel boats converge on the Sandbar each day to play with the resident stingrays in the shallow waters off Grand Cayman Island.

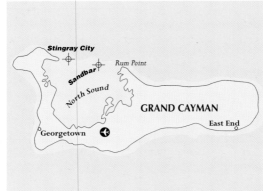

Stingray City and the Sandbar

Grand Cayman's Stingray City, and its counterpart, the Sandbar, have been featured in *National Geographic* and promoted worldwide on film, video and in magazine articles. This is possibly one of the most popular and impressive dive locations in the world. Dubbed 'the world's greatest 4m (13ft) dive', Stingray City is located inside the barrier reef along the north shore of Grand Cayman where the waters are virtually always sheltered and calm. Here, about 250 southern stingrays (*Dasyatis americana*) swoop in and envelop you in their 'wings' in their search for a free meal.

Divers are cautioned not to wear gloves when touching the stingrays, as the fabric can remove the protective mucus on the creature's leathery skin. Riding the stingrays, or grabbing them by the tail, is not recommended either as, if they feel threatened in any way, they may sting you.

At Stingray City the delicate balance between nature and enterprise is a curious mix and it is not really certain which of the two is ultimately in command of the situation. Suffice it to say that several hundred thousand tourists have enjoyed the delights of interacting with these creatures, and will hopefully continue to do so for many years to come.

Opposite Southern stingrays (*Dasyatis americana*) are so used to being hand fed that they will follow divers to the surface.

Left and above In the course of their constant search for tasty tidbits, stingrays often envelop divers in their wings.

Following pages Once the divers have finished feeding them, the stingrays quickly revert to their normal feeding behaviour – foraging in the sand for small crustaceans and molluscs.

Bloody Bay Wall

Wall diving is what brings so many people to Bloody Bay Wall, which is rated as the number one dive site of this kind in the Caribbean. Located to the north of Little Cayman, the wall begins at only 6–8m (20–27ft), allowing you all the time in the world to enjoy your dive at any depth you want, before it drops away to several hundred metres – well beyond the safe diving limit. Deeply undercut in some areas, the site is festooned with rope and barrel sponges, fabulous corals and a myriad fish. The shallows here are filled with coral canyons and also sand chutes, which lead you through spectacular caves into the pristine blue waters of the outer reef.

During the summer months, the coral canyons are home to millions of silverside minnows. From early summer through to September, there are literally thousands of these fish at several sites in the Cayman Islands. Inhabiting the deeper recesses of caves and canyons, silversides prefer areas with several exits, moving through them as a single entity in ever-changing shapes and forms. Jacks, tarpon and barracuda are usually seen in the vicinity of these massive shoals and can be observed closing in for the attack in what appears to be a highly strategic fashion: surrounding, herding and then rushing in for the kill.

It is not uncommon to have interactions with manta rays and eagle rays at Bloody Bay Wall. In fact, for a number of years, a manta ray known locally as Molly used to enthrall and entertain visitors with her spectacular aerial acrobatic feeding display.

Above Huge colourful sponges can be found in the Cayman Reefs, filtering nutrients from the current.

Left The independently moving eyes of the milk conch *(Strombus costatus)* are comical to watch.

Opposite The whitestar cardinalfish *(Apogon lachneri)* can often be found at night amidst sponges.

Greenhouse Reef

Greenhouse Reef, off the north shore of Cayman Brac, was chosen as the resting place of a former Russian destroyer. Renamed the MV *Captain Keith Tibbetts*, the 95m-long (316ft) vessel is a Brigadier type II class frigate, built in 1984 at Nadhodka in the USSR at a cost of US$30 million and weighing 1590 tons. Originally part of the old Soviet fleet stationed in Cuba during the Cold War, it was never actually involved in any conflict.

The location for the sinking was thoroughly examined by the local dive operators as well as the Cayman Islands Department of Environment, who also carried out the on-board inspection of the destroyer in order to determine her suitability as a dive site. The vessel lies inside the drop-off along the north wall of Cayman Brac at

Greenhouse Reef in depths of 20–30m (66–100ft), ensuring minimal environmental impact.

The MV *Captain Keith Tibbetts* lists only slightly to starboard, and is perfectly placed in a sand chute which plunges over the wall between two huge coral buttresses. There are healthy sections of coral on either side of the superstructure, carpeted with massive barrel sponges and, under the bow, at 25m (83ft), there is a field of garden eels (*Heteroconger halis*). Shortly after she sank, the vessel was surrounded by fish, leaving no doubt that she would soon be an integral part of reef life in the Caymans. Jean-Michel Cousteau, son of the late Jacques Cousteau, said that it 'is fitting that a vessel of destruction should become a flagship to marine conservation'.

Above Frigate No. 356 under tow from Cuba was given a total overhaul before her scheduled sinking.

Left The Jean-Michel Cousteau dive team carry out a photographic inspection right after her sinking.

Below The now renamed *Captain Keith Tibbetts* slips beneath the waves off Greenhouse Reef. Jean-Michel Cousteau was on board when she sank.

Map labels: Spot Bay; CAYMAN BRAC; Jennifer Bay; Russian Destroyer Greenhouse Reef; West End

CENTRAL AMERICA

Central America, the long finger of land connecting North and South America, was not only the land bridge for the migration and colonization of central Amerindian tribes in bygone days, but is also one of the routes taken by migrating birds. The countries which comprise this area are Mexico, Belize, Guatemala, Honduras, El Salvador, Nicaragua, Costa Rica and Panama.

Mexico's Caribbean coastline, Belize and Honduras feature principally for diving vacations. The barrier reef which runs north from Honduras to Cozumel (Mexico's only Caribbean island) is reputed to be the longest in the Caribbean and the second largest in the world, consisting of the largest natural coral atolls in the northern hemisphere, many of which are completely unexplored.

MEXICO'S CARIBBEAN COASTLINE

An Ancient Land Steeped in History

EL GRANDE CENOTE · NARCOSIS RIDGE · MANCHONES · SANTA ROSA WALL · PALANCAR REEF

Protruding like a giant thumb from the east coast of Mexico, the Yucatán Peninsula is a huge land mass that divides the Gulf of Mexico from the Caribbean Sea. The coastline of the Caribbean is bordered by the state of Quintana Roo, where sun worshippers and scuba divers abound. Though famous for its ancient Mayan ruins, such as Chichén Itzá, Coba and Tulum, nowadays the coral formations seem to outweigh the ancients as a drawcard. Besides splendid diving on living reefs, there are limestone caverns, or cenotes – carved out by centuries of climatic change – to explore.

'Cenote' is a Spanish corruption of the Mayan word for well, *tzenot*. Filled with the clearest water imaginable, these freshwater wells are part of the longest interconnecting underground cave system in the world. There are three registered centres for training in cave and cavern diving in the Yucatán. A requirement for this specialized course is a minimum of 14 cave dives with double tanks.

In 1969, a long sand bar shaped like the number '7' on the Caribbean coast emerged as 'the next Acapulco'. Nowadays, Cancún (pronounced 'Can-koon') is a 22.5km (14-mile), internationally recognized resort zone boasting stunning clean,

sandy beaches. The fish life found on Cancún's shallow offshore reefs is profuse and, in physical numbers, far exceeds the fish populations found further down the Yucatán coast.

Some 30km (19 miles) from Cancún is Cozumel, Mexico's largest Caribbean island. It is 47km (29 miles) long, 15km (9 miles) wide, shaped like a drop-jewel, and covered in large part by dense jungle and swamps. It also has several Mayan ruins. Tectonic movements gave birth to this submarine plateau, which was quickly colonized by coral formations in the shallower range of the ridge. Because of melting glaciers, the sea level rose about 30m (100ft). This generated a vertical growth of the coral reef and created perpendicular barriers around the original sea mount. Now there is a classic example of a petrified, or 'ironstone', shoreline with live coral fringing reefs offshore.

The diving along the southwest reefs and shoals of Cozumel is world class. Virtually all of the diving is drift diving by boat and, depending on your level of skill and experience, the dive guides will escort you to the most suitable site. Diving by boat is generally accompanied, but you are able to shore dive on your own at a number of different locations along the island's west coast.

Best time to go The sea is most calm from May–Sep, giving rise to the clearest water conditions. For cenote diving, Nov–Mar are peak months for water clarity.

Climate Rainfall is pronounced from Apr–May when the eastern trade winds blow; during Sep–Jan there is a chance of hurricanes and high humidity. In Jun–Sep air temperatures rise to 30–40°C (80–90°F).

Getting there There are international air connections to Cancún and Cozumel. Internal flights link Cancún to Chichén Itzá and there is a regular ferry service from Puerto Morelos and Playa Del Carmen linking the Yucatán mainland with Cozumel.

Special interest Visit the ancient Mayan ruins of Chichén Itzá, Coba and Tulum.

Accommodation and dive operations Dive Paradise has arrangements with many of the hotels; the Dive Shop works with the Fiesta Americana on Cozumel. Quicksilver and Manta Divers have arrangements with a variety of establishments in Cancún. Cedam Divers and Aquatec are some of your best bets for cenote diving in the area around Akumal.

Emergency information All the diving operations on Cozumel and in Cancún administer a US$1 charge per diver. This money goes towards the upkeep of the recompression chamber on Cozumel and also towards the treatment costs of anyone using the chamber. Tel: (52 987) 20140, 22387 or 21430.

Previous pages The sunset when seen from the outer coral atolls off Belize is always spectacular.
Opposite Yellow tube sponges (*Aplysina fistularis*) stretch out into the Caribbean current off the Yucatán.
Top The brilliant orange elephant's ear sponge (*Agelas clathrodes*) is the largest found in Mexican waters.

El Grande Cenote

El Grande Cenote is a massive, circular, collapsed cavern, where the former surface is now a low plug of limestone and swampy areas covered in lilies and scrubby water-loving trees. Over 60m (200ft) across, this huge sink hole has dropped 6m (20ft) below ground level and access to the dive is down a rickety set of rough wooden ladders. A muddy path takes you to the edge of the vertical limestone wall and you can quite clearly see the cave system stretching away in front of you.

While paddling over the lilies (which also make a great photographic subject) you quickly drop down to about 12m (40ft) amidst some spectacular limestone columns, stalactites, stalagmites and numerous other limestone structures. Visibility is exceptional – you are still able to see a snorkeller at the entrance to the cavern when over 60m (200ft) underground. A protective suit and hood are recommended at all times, as the freshwater temperature is about 10°F cooler than its saltwater counterpart.

Below left A diver is framed against the massive entrance of Carwash Cenote near Akumal.

Below right An underwater pillar reveals that the cave was once on dry land.

Opposite Divers negotiate the entrance to the cenote amidst the remains of fallen trees.

THE FORMATION OF CENOTES

More than 250 million years ago, the entire central American continent was underwater. As time passed, the sea level dropped and ultimately left a shallow, raised plateau of soft, porous limestone. This bedrock composition is susceptible to erosion, and the severe tropical rainstorms over the centuries created huge underground caverns. A cenote is formed when the roof of one of these vast caverns collapses, revealing a natural well.

The great Mayan cities were all built around cenotes. The people regarded them as sacred, and gifts and sacrifices were thrown into many of the wells. The great Cenote Sagrado at Chichén Itzá has yielded great wealth and its 20m (66ft) depths are off limits to divers.

In the south of the country, near Chetumal, is Cenote Azul. At 100m (330ft), it is the deepest known cenote in Mexico. But the most famous of all is Nohoch Nah Chich, discovered by Mike Madden in 1987. Some 50km (30 miles) of caves and passageways have been explored and charted in this cavern system. Around 50 of the cenotes are found along the Akumal-Tulum Corridor, 100km (62 miles) south of the holiday resort of Cancún. All are well mapped, but still not completely explored.

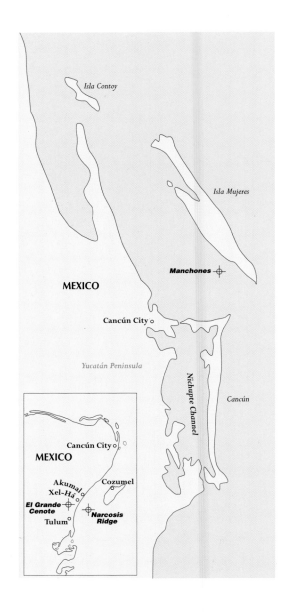

If you look upwards along the reef, you will usually be able to see a moving fringe of creole wrasse (*Clepticus parrai*) mixed with rather glum-looking blue chromis (*Chromis cyanea*). Amid the coral and sponge branches you will also find hamlets, basslets, parrotfish and moray eels. As with all deep dives, take note of your time at each depth to allow for safe diving limits and to avoid decompression stops on the way to the surface.

Manchones

It takes approximately 30 minutes by boat from Cancún to reach this series of small, low-lying reefs near Isla Mujeres in Isla Mujeres Bay. Suitable for both diving and snorkelling, this site differs from some of the other locations in the area in that it consists primarily of a series of coral bommies, or patch reefs, instead of the usual strip reef. Manchones is a reliable area for sightings of large shoals of several Caribbean fish species, as well as a greater than average number of queen angelfish (*Holacanthus ciliaris*) of all sizes and ages, the juveniles being every bit as brilliantly coloured as the adults. Small redspotted hawkfish (*Amblycirrhitus pinos*) dot the reefs, their comical stance attracting divers' attention. Dive guides tend to take you on a somewhat circuitous route amidst the coral formations; at night, the same site is an excellent learning curve, with the true colours of the Caribbean Sea revealing themselves under the glare of torchlight. Hermit crabs, arrow crabs, octopus, and toadfish all come out at night and wander around the reefs.

Narcosis Ridge

Due to the extreme depth of the dive, the name refers to Nitrogen Narcosis, a malady often called 'Rapture of the Deep', which divers pressing beyond 30m (100ft) are likely to experience. The ridge is an extended coral spur which juts out much more than the rest of the surrounding reef. From the start of the wall at around 18m (60ft) the reef drops steeply to 37m (120 ft) and then drops once more off the continental shelf to way beyond the safe limits of recreational scuba diving. There are large boulder star corals which reduce in size the further you descend into a world of sponges covering the walls. Always remember to look outwards and below you into the blue as there is an excellent chance you will see turtles and other large pelagics.

Santa Rosa Wall

Past Palancar Reef, Santa Rosa Wall is the next major reef system you will encounter as you travel in a northerly direction along the edge of the western continental shelf of Cozumel. Similar in size to Palancar, the reef is so large that it is always treated as a drift dive when the tide is running at its strongest. Having dived this reef several times, I can honestly say that each time I visit the area, I do not recognize the reef – it

Left The star-eye hermit crab *(Dardanus venosus)* carries its 'mobile home', a discarded conch shell.

Previous pages The queen angelfish *(Holacanthus ciliaris)* is widespread along the Mexican coast.

changes so much according to the depth and the location of the starting point of your dive.

The inner (shallower) reef is similar to Palancar Shallows, with huge areas of corals made up of species which enjoy fast-moving currents, such as wide-mesh sea fans (*Gorgonia mariae*), sea plumes (*Pseudopterogorgia bipinnata*) and sea rods (*Plexaurella nutans*). This whole section is rather untidy in appearance due to the profusion of algae which covers the entire reef, pushing out the corals and sponges. The mid-section of the reef at the start of the steep slope has some lovely huge caverns and swim-throughs, very similar to sections of Bloody Bay Wall in Little Cayman Island; here you can swim under huge coral outcrops which gradually make their way to the edges of the outer wall or drop-off. The outer reaches of the reef change shape yet again, with much of the

coral wall becoming vertical in profile, dropping 70m (230 ft) before it reaches another ancient sea bed sand slope, testimony to the changes in the depths which have created so many of the mainland's tunnels and cenotes.

The predominant reef forms are the sponges. The largest branching specimens are the brown tube (*Agelas conifera*) and stove-pipe sponges (*Aplysina archeri*); other large groupings are *Pseudoceratina crassa* and the yellow tube sponge (*Aplysina fistularis*). Divers take great delight at weaving their way amongst the massive coral buttresses which make up this outer wall, but time at depth is

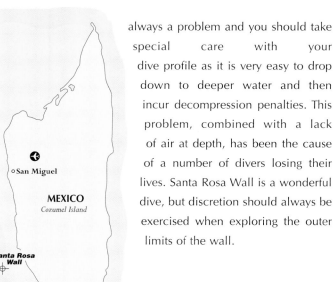

always a problem and you should take special care with your dive profile as it is very easy to drop down to deeper water and then incur decompression penalties. This problem, combined with a lack of air at depth, has been the cause of a number of divers losing their lives. Santa Rosa Wall is a wonderful dive, but discretion should always be exercised when exploring the outer limits of the wall.

Above At Manchones in Isla Mujeres Bay, a school of snappers hovers under a coral overhang to take full advantage of the protection it offers.

Palancar Reef

Palancar is a popular reef. The Cozumel Dive Association members always treat this area as a drift dive and, depending on the strength of the current and the number of other dive boats in the vicinity, divers will be dropped into the water at any point of a wide number of locations.

Palancar Shallows, a separate reef, is perhaps the most extensive structure with depths as shallow as 3m (10ft) in some areas, reaching over 18m (60ft) at the edge of the wall before sloping steeply away over a wide sand plain to the next reef.

This section of Palancar is cut by sand chutes which have created narrow coral canyons and thousands of overhangs. These form convoluted caves where the hanging vine (*Halimeda goreaui*) gives vivid splashes of green to the otherwise dull colours of the reef. It is always a good idea to carry a torch on this dive as lobster and file clams (*Lima lima* and *L. scabra*) invariably hide in the dark recesses.

To the south of Palancar Shallows is the Horse-shoe, an amphitheatre cut out of an otherwise featureless wall. There are huge barrel sponges (*Xestospongia muta*) and some rare black coral (*Antipathes* spp.) on the lower slopes. Graham's sheet coral (*Agaricia grahamae*) forms under-hanging holes, and wire corals (*Cirrhipathes leutkeni*) spiral into the depths. To the north the reef slopes upwards to Palancar Caves, a site usually visited at the same time. Because of the varied profile of the reef, you can start the dive very deep at the Horseshoe and ascend to the shallow sections which come to within 6m (20ft) of the surface. The reef here is more convoluted in shape, with coral canyons and small caves. Fish are sparse, besides black groupers (*Mycteroperca bonaci*), yellowtail snappers (*Ocyurus chrysurus*) and the small shoals of *Chromis* and creole wrasse that occur in the shallows.

Experienced divers favour Palancar Deep, at the outer edge of the continental shelf forming the deep water channel between Cozumel and the Yucatán mainland. A raised ridge of corals and sponges has created an incredible display of coral forms, caves and canyons.

Opposite The very colourful red hind *(Epinephelus guttatus)* is one of the smaller groupers.

Below Huge boulder corals *(Montastrea annularis)* form the major coral buttresses at Palancar Reef.

BELIZE

The Caribbean's Largest Barrier Reef

TURNEFFE ISLAND ATOLL · GLOVER'S REEF · LIGHTHOUSE REEF AND THE BLUE HOLE

Best time to go The climate is subtropical and the air temperature averages around 26°C (80°F) throughout the year. The driest months are from Nov–May, when easterly winds predominate.

Getting there There are flights on Taca, Continental and American Airlines from all the major US hub airports, as well as other flights from South America, Honduras and Puerto Rico.

Special interest The live-aboard dive boats *Belize Aggressor III*, *Wave Dancer*, *Manta IV* and *Rembrandt van Rijn* all operate around the offshore reefs and atolls, and specialize in trips to the Blue Hole, Turneffe Island and Lighthouse Reef.

Accommodation and dive operations Turneffe Island Lodge is located at the southernmost tip of Cay Bokel; Glover Reef Resort and Manta Reef Resort are well established on Glover's Reef. Lighthouse Reef Resort is located on Big Northern Cay. Coral Cay Conservation run their research centre from Calabash Bay and they also host projects all over the Belize coastline and island reefs.

Electrical supply American-style plugs, 110V at 60 cycles.

Emergency information The closest recompression chamber is in Belize City. There is an emergency helicopter service operating from the outer atolls. Tel: 90 for assistance. Divers' Alert Network (DAN), tel: (919) 648 8111.

Formerly referred to as the Mosquito Coast, Belize was first inhabited by emigrants from the British colony of Jamaica, who established a thriving timber industry, harvesting mahogany and other hardwood trees. Known as 'the Baymen', these early settlers resisted several attacks by the Spanish over the centuries, until eventually, in 1862, the region was annexed to Jamaica and came under British rule. British Honduras, as it was then known, finally became an independent state and member of the Commonwealth in 1981. Located between Mexico to the north and Guatemala and Honduras to the south, the country appears to have been custom-made for diving, with the second-largest barrier reef in the world (the largest in the Caribbean) located just a few kilometres from the mainland. Couple that with three massive coral atolls – Turneffe Island Atoll, Lighthouse Reef and Glover's Reef – and it's easy to understand Belize's status as a world-class diving destination.

Belize City, although not an ideal destination for tourists, is the starting point for exploring many of the ancient Mayan ruins that are dotted about the country, the most visually impressive being Lamanai, on the shores of the New River lagoon. The closest ruins to Belize City are Altun-Ha, situated only 62km (38 miles) away. Numerous nature parks have been created in Belize, and at least one should be included in any field trip to the country; the largest is the Rio Bravo Conservation Area, at 100,000ha (250,000 acres).

Belize is also home to a reef ecology project that was set up by Coral Cay Conservation, with the help of the Belize Coastal Zone Management Authority and the University College of Belize. Volunteers are exploring, mapping and recording the marine life habitats of Turneffe Island Atoll, one of the most important biological systems in the Caribbean and characterized by lush mangroves, littoral palm forests and pristine coral reefs with elusive manatees, playful dolphins and other fabulous marine life. The volunteers, who are all given instruction on the collection of scientific data and who aim to survey forests, lagoons and reefs throughout the 350km² (210-square-mile) area of Turneffe Atoll, form part of a national drive to establish an effective management plan for the protection and sustainable use of the atoll's outstanding biodiversity.

Offshore on Lighthouse Reef you will find a massive oceanic blue hole which is over 300m (1000ft) across. If you were to dive around the perimeter of this incredible natural feature you would come across some huge stalactites suspended from the ceilings of the side passageways. Unfortunately these are all in very deep water, and there is little time for further exploration as you may incur decompression penalties.

Opposite This diver is in danger of touching the sponge – vulnerable marine life should never be touched.

Top A bottlenose dolphin *(Tursiops truncatus)* swims over eelgrass beds in a lagoon off Belize's coral atolls.

Turneffe Island Atoll

The largest of the three coral atolls in Belize is Turneffe Island, the only atoll to have a mangrove forest covering much of the inner shoreline of the cays which make up the north–south-aligned reef system. Most diving is confined to the southern-most point, known as the Elbow. Reefs running to the northwest are shallower with a gently sloping wall, while those to the northeast are spectacularly vertical. Since the walls start at 18m (60ft) and there is a greater likelihood of currents, these are regarded as dives for the experienced.

The shallower sites have luxurious coral growth with sand channels and patches between them, and virtually every part of the reef has overhangs and small caves where blackbar soldierfish (*Myripristis jacobus*) live alongside glasseye snappers (*Priacanthus cruenatus*). Banded coral shrimps (*Stenopus hispidus*) attend to the fish that queue to be cleaned of parasites. In 1983 the 15m-long (50ft) wooden hulled transport vessel *Sayanora* was deliberately sunk amidst these coral heads as an artificial reef and is now home to all manner of fish and invertebrates.

To the east, on the deeper slopes, huge coral buttresses have become a classic but massively proportioned spur-and-groove formation. This is indented with canyons and fissures and it is also smothered in soft and hard corals, sea fans, plumes, rods and sponges, all thriving together with a huge and diverse population of fish.

Glover's Reef

Glover's Reef is part of the southernmost atoll in Belize, and offers a huge variety of dive sites off the string of sand cays which make up the perimeter of the atoll. The shallows are dominated by huge stands of elkhorn coral (*Acropora palmata*) and simply massive pillar coral (*Dendrogyra cylindrus*). The lagoon covers 130km^2 (80 square miles) and reaches a maximum depth of 15m (50ft).

Left These tiny social featherduster worms (*Bispira brunnea*) are light and pressure sensitive, making them rather difficult to photograph.

It contains over 700 separate coral heads, all of which are perfect for safe, easy snorkelling and photography. The virtually impenetrable barrier reef wall starts at 9m (30ft) and drops vertically in many places to over 600m (2000ft).

Large groupers are common, as are manta rays, dolphins, spotted eagle rays and turtles. Few of the live-aboard dive boats in Belize venture this far south, as there is such good diving around the other atolls and the barrier reef. Consequently, not much of this small atoll has been explored, and there are many discoveries still to be made.

Lighthouse Reef and the Blue Hole

Originally known (from the 1750s onwards) as the Eastern Reefs, Lighthouse Reef is situated some 65km (40 miles) east of Belize City. It was later named after the lighthouse built on Half Moon Cay in 1820. The first lighthouse was replaced in 1848 and, in 1931, a steel-framed platform and tower was erected. Modern technology has since overtaken the old lighthouse, and today it is solar-powered.

Half Moon Cay is the first marine conservation area to be established in Belize, and it is also a bird sanctuary for large numbers of red-footed boobies. To the south of Half Moon Cay is the shallow lagoon of the atoll; along its northern shore there is a drop-off where most of the diving is concentrated. The reef here is superb with a hanging garden of rope sponges (*Aplysina caulifrons* and *Aplysina fulva*), and tiny zoanthids (minute colonial hydroids similar to cup corals) that grow on thin rope sponges, green finger sponges and brown tube sponges. Beneath every overhang can be found the hanging vine (*Halimeda copiosa*). Lighthouse Reef is a riot of colour, thanks particularly to the large numbers of brightly coloured angelfish, parrotfish, wrasse and *Chromis*.

The legendary Blue Hole, in the centre of the atoll, is an almost perfect circle, 300m (1000ft) in diameter. The edge of the vertical wall starts in only 2–5m (6–17ft) of water and then plummets 124m (412ft). At 43m (140ft), where the wall ends, there is a cavern of massive proportions with gigantic stalactites indicating that this was once above sea level. The guided dive of Blue Hole, which is for experienced divers only, will take you around stalactites that are over 5m (17ft) in diameter and 18m (60ft) long – simply breathtaking.

Above Juvenile green turtles *(Chelonia mydas)* occur near the barrier reef forming Belize's atolls.

Top Tiny lightbulb tunicates *(Clavelina picta)* cling to the stem of a yellow sponge.

Right Strawberry sponges *(Mycale laxissima)* grow over the stems of black corals *(Antipathes* spp.).

BAY ISLANDS

A Macrophotographer's Dream

JADO TRADER WRECK • GUANAJA'S WEST POINT • EEL'S GARDEN • ROATAN'S WEST POINT
LITTLE COCO AND MARJORIE'S BANK • PELICAN POINT

The Bay Islands are 64km (40 miles) north of Honduras and comprise the three large islands of Roatan, Guanaja and Utila together with a few smaller satellites, such as Barbareta. Also part of the Bay Islands is a smaller island group, just a short distance from the mainland, called Cayos Cochinos, as well as a series of raised sea mounts between this group and Roatan. All the islands are coralline in origin, but were forced upwards by volcanic upheaval and are now covered in lush vegetation; the shoreline is still ancient coral-reef limestone.

Originally settled by the Payan Indians, a close relation of the Maya who dominated much of central America, the local population was decimated by enslavement and disease introduced by the Spanish. English settlers brought agriculture to the islands before they were eventually ceded to Honduras. Although there is a legacy of British influence throughout the Bay Islands, the language and customs of the islanders are being influenced once more by the Spanish as mainland Hondurans migrate to the islands in search of work and a gentler way of life.

The wonderful abundance of the region's marine life, together with visibility that is consistently over 30m (100ft), has made the Bay Islands increasingly popular with divers.

Roatan has a lush, mountainous ridge running its entire length of 58km (36 miles); it is the largest

of the islands. Possibly the best way to explore its dive sites is with the *Bay Islands Aggressor III*, a live-aboard boat based at French Harbour which also includes the submarine sea mounts and Cayos Cochinos in its charters.

Located to the east of Roatan, Guanaja is only about 15km long (9 miles). It is a mountainous island with a fringe of palm trees and pine-clad hills. With no road infrastructure, all transportation is undertaken by water taxis and small outboard-engine-powered boats.

In some places, the vertical wall of the island's heavy barrier reef only starts 5m (16ft) from the surface. The reef, which is over 100m (330ft) wide, is bisected by three deep channels that have created large, sheltered inner lagoons rich in corals and fish. Along the southern reef tract, the wreck of the *Jado Trader* lies in about 32m (107ft) of water.

The smallest island, Utila, is situated to the west of Roatan and is much flatter with huge, mature mangrove forests. With little rainwater run-off, the waters here are thought to be cleaner and clearer than elsewhere in the Bay Islands, and there is a greater chance of seeing whale sharks here too.

Cayos Cochinos, often referred to as the Hog Islands, is a small, emerald string of islands and cays lying just 19km (12 miles) from the mainland. It is regarded as one of the top locations in the Caribbean for macrophotography.

Best time to go
Diving is excellent throughout the year, but Apr–May and Oct–Nov are traditionally rainy periods. Oct–Nov may also have rougher seas, which can be awkward on a live-aboard boat, although the captain always moors up in sheltered bays. Water temperatures average 26°C (80°F) and air temperatures rarely rise above 32°C (90°F).

Getting there
Taca, Continental and American airlines all have daily flights to San Pedro Sula on mainland Honduras from Miami, Houston and New Orleans. A transfer on Air Islena is necessary from Honduras to Roatan. Be warned, these are 16-seater aircraft and excess baggage may be a problem. A lesser service also operates direct from Roatan to Houston.

Special interest
The Roatan Institute for Marine Sciences is at Anthony's Key Resort and has a maritime museum as well as daily dolphin shows. Live-aboard boats include the *Wind Dancer* and the 33m (110ft) *Bay Islands Aggressor III*. The latter accommodates a total of 16 passengers and five crew in luxury. Operating from Romeo's Hotel and Restaurant, French Harbour, since 1990, the boat's crew have pinpointed some of the best sites in the Bay Islands.

Emergency information
The recompression chamber is situated on Roatan and is operated by St Luke's Mission. Visiting divers are requested to pay US$1 per day towards its upkeep. Tel/fax: (504) 45 1515; tel/fax (24 hours): (504) 45 1500. Diver's Alert Network (DAN), tel: (919) 648 8111.

Opposite Sunlight dapples a huge brain coral in the shallow reefs off Cayos Cochinos in the Bay Islands.
Top The *Bay Islands Aggressor III* is seen here anchored off Cayos Cochinos, a popular diving destination.

Jado Trader Wreck

The *Jado Trader*, a derelict freighter that was sunk deliberately in 1987 off the southern reef, approximately 1.6km (1 mile) offshore from Guanaja, now lies on her starboard side at a depth of 33m (110ft). The wreck is nestled between steeply sided coral pinnacles – the one facing her bow is conical in shape. Due to the depth of the freighter, the dive plan is to spend around 20 minutes on the wreck and the remaining time degassing on the surrounding reef before returning to the dive boat.

Even in the short time that the ship has been underwater, it has become well encrusted with marine growth, including colourful sponges, hydroids and corals. There are two large, green moray eels on the wreck that are used to inquisitive divers and often come quite close to you.

Several large groupers also inhabit the wreck and approach divers very quickly, giving the impression that they have been fed in the past, although the practice is frowned upon.

The wreck's masts and rigging are intact, heavily encrusted in sponges and deep-water gorgonians. A school of silverside minnows hides in part of the hold and various groupers linger nearby, waiting to catch the unwary. Due to the prolific fish life on the wreck (such as smaller wrasse, parrotfish, filefish, angel- and butterflyfish), the wreck is also visited by black jacks (*Caranx lugubris*) as well as horse-eyed jacks (*Caranx latus*), which stream in from the blue to eye the local population of wreck dwellers.

Below The *Jado Trader*, still intact and covered in marine growth, rests between two coral heads.

Above This winch on the foredeck of the *Jado Trader* is covered in colourful encrusting sponges.

Guanaja's West Point

Named after its location towards the western point of Guanaja, the reef wall starts fairly close to shore at around 9m (30ft) and curls over before dropping into the depths. The lip of the wall is split open by several deeply incised canyons that can quite easily be negotiated and are always filled with a number of very interesting marine species. From the *Aggressor*'s mooring buoy, travel to your right, always keeping the reef wall to your left, until you come across a small under-sea island of coral standing separately from the reef wall. Here you will find huge deep-water gorgonians and black corals, as well as whip corals spiralling upwards, and simply massive sponges everywhere. This site is also a superb night dive with many pufferfish hiding inside sponges, some cryptic teardrop crabs and lots of octopus.

BAY ISLANDS
Roatan Island
Port Royal
Oak Ridge
French Harbour
Coxen Hole
Eel's Garden
West Point

Eel's Garden

Eel's Garden, located towards the southeastern point of Roatan, is named after a large colony of garden eels (*Heteroconger halis*) which inhabit the sand plain. Here you will also find peacock flounders (*Bothus lunatus*), as well as helmet gurnard (*Dactylopterus volitans*) and spotted scorpionfish (*Scorpaena plumieri*). The reef wall has very few of the more common sea fans found elsewhere in the Caribbean and only a few common sea plumes, but the deep wall incisions more than make up for this with brilliantly coloured rope sponges, tube sponges, delicate

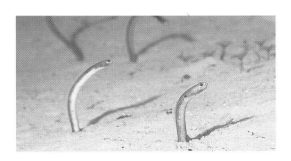

black corals and angular sea whips (*Pterogorgia anceps*). At night, the tops of all the corals are straddled by giant basket stars (*Astrophyton muricatum*) and virtually every sponge and sea fan has its carpet of brittle starfish (*Ophiothrix suensonii*). The anemones have their attendant cleaning shrimps, and filefish and pufferfish nestle into sponges for safety.

Roatan's West Point

West Point is another superb site that is more popular as a night dive. It is not as steep as other walls, having a gentle slope that rises into quite shallow water. There are gulleys and canyons everywhere and they are all topped with soft and hard corals, dotted with cleaning gobies and ever-moving groups of bluehead wrasse (*Thalassoma bifasciatum*). Spotted drum (*Equetus punctatus*) are more than evident, as are several moray eels (*Gymnothorax funebris*) and the sharptail snake eel (*Myrichthys breviceps*), which forages among the surrounding coral rubble for small crustaceans.

Little Coco and Marjorie's Bank

The group of open-ocean sea mounts between Roatan and Cayos Cochinos runs parallel to the shore; the smallest is Little Coco, the largest Marjorie's Bank. Both have similar dive profiles, with the top of the reef at around 15m (50ft) and the drop-off starting at around 24m (80ft). There is a good chance of encountering turtles, barracuda and big schools of everything, including horse-eyed jacks (*Caranx latus*), black jacks (*Caranx lugubris*) and Atlantic spadefish (*Chaetodipterus faber*). At certain times of year, ocean triggerfish (*Canthidermis sufflamen*) can be seen in mating pairs, excavating nests in the sand patches amid the corals on the reef. Nurse sharks and Caribbean

reef sharks are fairly common and, on most trips to Cayos Cochinos, there are sightings of dolphins riding the bow wave of the *Aggressor*.

Pelican Point

At Cayos Cochinos's Pelican Point the reef crest is only 3m (10ft) from the surface after which it plummets down a wall with numerous canyons, overhangs and caves. The shallows behind the reef crest are home to sailfin blennies (*Emblemaria pandionis*), yellowhead jawfish (*Opistognathus aurifrons*) and plumed scorpionfish (*Scorpaena grandicornis*). In the evening you might encounter a manta ray, spiralling around as it feeds on plankton. Creole wrasse swarm over the reef crest, and parrotfish, snapper and grunt are everywhere. There are flamingo tongue snails on virtually every sea fan, and angelfish are two a penny.

At night, this site takes on another dimension when giant clinging crabs (*Mithrax spinosissimus*) live up to their name, clinging halfway up the purple sea fans that rise and fall in the current. Octopus are extremely approachable, sitting on the coral heads, while tiny flatworms slither over the sand and golden stingrays (*Urolophus jamaicensis*) search for tidbits. Orange ball anemones are fairly common and many of the sea whips and rods are surrounded by colourful nudibranchs or sea slugs vying for space with brittle starfish, teardrop crabs and basket stars.

Little Coco
Marjorie's Bank
BAY ISLANDS
Cayos Cochinos (Hog Islands)
Pelican Point

Top Coming out only at night, this magnificent sea urchin (*Astropyga magnifica*) perches amid fire coral.

Left Garden eels (*Heteroconger halis*) can be found in the sand plains, 'pecking' at passing plankton.

DUTCH ANTILLES

The Dutch Antilles comprise Aruba, Curaçao, Bonaire, Sint Maarten, Saba and St Eustatius, though the latter two are included in the Leeward Islands section of this book (see page 92). Aruba, Bonaire and Curaçao, or the ABCs as they are collectively known, are situated off the north coast of Venezuela. Curaçao and Bonaire are both low-lying and covered in dense vegetation.

The islands have some of the best diving in the Caribbean, particularly for macrophotography and especially in shallow water, and are famed for their massive pipe sponges (*Aplysina* spp.). The vertical walls close to the shore allow for short boat rides and also for doing shore dives as an alternative to escorted dives. The islands boast 24-hour diving, and that is exactly what you will want to do.

BONAIRE AND CURAÇAO

Frogfish, Sea Horses and Wonderful Corals

SALT PIER AND TOWN PIER • *HILMA HOOKER* WRECK • CAPTAIN DON'S HABITAT • YELLOWMAN • ROCKPILE • *SUPERIOR PRODUCER* WRECK • BEACON POINT • MUSHROOM FOREST • *TUGBOAT* WRECK

Bonaire was discovered in 1499 by a Spanish expedition led by Alonso de Ojeda, and was originally known as Isla de Brasil, or 'island of dyewood', after the indigenous population of Amerindians who used the dye from these trees in their rock paintings. The Dutch acquired Curaçao in 1634, and Bonaire and Aruba in 1636, thereby consolidating their position in the Caribbean. They started producing salt in Curaçao in 1639.

Bonaire became autonomous from Holland in 1954 and, together with Curaçao (excluding Aruba), became a territory of the Kingdom of the Netherlands in 1986. The mix of English, Dutch, Spanish, Portuguese, and Indian has created a unique Creole dialect called *papiamento*, with Dutch being the next major local language and American-English now being adopted for tourists.

Bonaire is 50km (30 miles) east of Curaçao and 80km (50 miles) north of Venezuela. The 38km-long (28-mile) island is aligned in a northwesterly direction, making the west coast and the satellite island of Klein Bonaire perfectly situated and sheltered from the predominant trade winds. Klein Bonaire and Bonaire are fringed with superb coral reefs, which mostly drop near-vertically into the depths, making them accessible from the shore. Klein Bonaire is roughly circular in shape and can only be reached by boat (a five-minute ride).

Bonaire's picturesque capital, Kralendijk, is full of Dutch architecture. The main pier, Town Pier, is a popular night diving site. The importance of diving tourism to Bonaire's economy is such that the entire island has been declared a marine reserve and all visiting divers must attend an orientation course. Your first dive is always on a 'house reef' accessed from the shore so that the dive instructor can check your buoyancy before you embark on a boat dive to one of the more delicate and pristine coral sites.

Curaçao is 62km (38 miles) long and 11km (7 miles) wide, and is the largest of the ABCs. A huge oil-refining industry overshadows the arid beauty of the island and the capital, Willemstad, is quite commercialized with numerous cruise ship facilities. Shopping is superb, however, and the town has an appealing European atmosphere.

Orientated in an east–west direction, Curaçao is susceptible to easterly trade winds, making diving rougher than Bonaire. Nonetheless, the reefs are on a par with Bonaire and marine life is equally profuse. There are two superb wrecks in Curaçao, the *Superior Producer*, in deep water, and the *Tugboat*, which lies in very shallow water. Curaçao is home to a new aquarium exhibit where divers can enjoy an underwater experience with sharks and tarpon. The island also has the most anemones and shrimps in the Caribbean.

Best time to go Most rain falls May–Nov, but the islands are outside the hurricane belt, making them a pretty safe choice.

Getting there Regular international flights from Europe, the USA and South America to Curaçao and Bonaire; Curaçao is a major airport in the area, so most flights to Bonaire are routed through Curaçao by Antillean Airline (ALM). Be warned: there is a strict baggage limit on all ALM flights of only 20kg (44 lb) per person.

Special interest Visit the Old Market in Willemstad, Curaçao. Washington–Slagbaai National Park in Bonaire is interesting, particularly at Playa Funchi where lizards eat out of your hand.

Accommodation and dive operations Underwater Curaçao is at Lion's Dive Hotel and Marina, east of Willemstad. Peter Hughes Diving is at Princess Beach Hotel. All West Diving and Adventures are at All West Apartments. Captain Don's Habitat, which has opened its second base along the west shore of Curaçao, is located along the same strip of land that includes Sand Dollar Condominium Resort, Lion's Dive Hotel and Harbour Village Beach Resort.

Electricity supply American-style plugs, 110V.

Emergency information The Curaçao Recompression Chamber is at St Elizabeth Hospital, tel: 110. The Bonaire Foundation Recompression Chamber is at the San Francisco Hospital, tel: 8900.

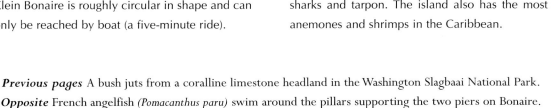

Previous pages A bush juts from a coralline limestone headland in the Washington Slagbaai National Park.
Opposite French angelfish *(Pomacanthus paru)* swim around the pillars supporting the two piers on Bonaire.
Top You can safely feed the nurse sharks in the Curaçao Aquarium through a series of feeding ports.

Salt Pier and Town Pier

Bonaire's two piers make exceptional dives and should not be missed. Town Pier has always been a favourite with local dive shops, but access is limited as the dock is in constant use. The site is therefore chosen for night dives only, and then only at short notice, midweek. Unfortunately, most of the dive boats end up at the pier at the same time and, although the sponges which cover the pier's support pilings are an outrageous combination of colours, the area can become somewhat like a zoo with torch-wielding divers moving everywhere and getting in each other's way. However, the photographic results can far outweigh any discomfort experienced. There are also resident orange sea horses, trumpetfish, hermit crabs and fireworms, all of which just add to the dizzying colour of the sponges.

The Salt Pier to the south of the island is another matter. Used much less frequently, the pier can be dived by day or night directly from the shore, but does involve a swim of about 100m (330ft) to get out to the deeper parts of the pilings which support the old pier. During the day the pier is often home to a simply gigantic shoal of bigeye scad (*Selar crumenophthalmus*), known on Curaçao as *Mas Bongos*. They are so vast in numbers that at times you cannot see the support legs of the pier, which are over 12m (49ft) high and span 30m (100ft) across. At night, the pier is awash with colour: old ropes and cables are like garlands of flowers, covered in cup corals. Everywhere you look there are brilliantly coloured sponges, crawling with crustaceans, nudibranchs and fireworms.

Above left The Salt Pier to the south of Bonaire is quite possibly the best all-round dive on the island.

Left The huge colourful sponges on the pier's pilings make superb photographic subjects.

Below These aggregations of bigeye scad, locally known as *Mas Bongos*, can literally blot out the sun.

Washington-Slagbaai National Park

BONAIRE

Yellowman
KLEIN BONAIRE
Captain Don's Habitat

Kralendijk
Rockpile
Town Pier
Hilma Hooker Wreck

Salt Pier

Hilma Hooker Wreck

The *Hilma Hooker* was a former drug runner's cargo ship which broke down en route to the USA. Hunted for several years, it had changed names at least 30 times in an attempt to elude the Drug Enforcement Agency before it experienced mechanical rudder failure and had to sail close to Bonaire. She was taken in tow to the Town Pier, where customs officers boarded her and discovered that all the crew had managed to escape, except for the cook. The ship was impounded and, once her cargo of 11,340kg (25,000 lb) of drugs had been removed and destroyed, she was deliberately sunk as an artificial reef to the south of the island on 12 September 1984.

She now lies on her starboard side, her bows pointing south in 27m (90ft) of water. Marine growth has been slow on the ship, but gradually she is becoming home to sponges, hard and soft corals and huge numbers of fish, including a couple of resident tarpon (*Megalops atlanticus*).

Above The *Hilma Hooker* rests on her starboard side in 27m (90ft) of water to the south of Bonaire.

Right The massive rudder and propeller of the *Hilma Hooker* dwarf this passing diver.

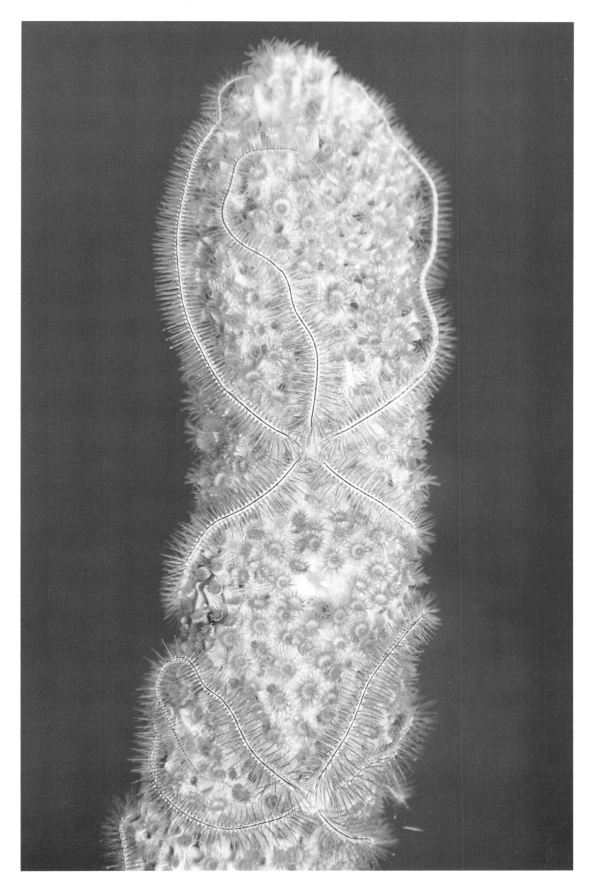

Above Brittle starfish *(Ophiothrix suensonii)* clamber out onto soft corals at night to feed.

Left The roughhead blenny *(Acanthemblemaria aspera)* hides in deserted tube worm holes for added protection.

Rockpile

On the other side of Klein Bonaire is Rockpile, comprising a number of sites lying close together. Although it has a rather unattractive name, the site is a mass of different hard and soft corals, sea fans, plumes and thousands of sponges all gathered on a steeply sloping wall which plunges into the depths. This is also home to another of the rarer Caribbean inhabitants, the longlure frogfish (*Antennarius multiocellatus*), which blends in so perfectly with the surrounding sponges and corals that it is virtually impossible to find unless you use dive lights during the day. The light may disturb it, causing it to move, but more often the colours are different when illuminated, for instance, yellow: in bright torchlight you can see that the yellow of the fish is more striking than the yellow of the coral. Frogfish use a lure which they dangle in front of their cavernous mouths to attract unwary blennies and small wrasse.

Left Elkhorn corals *(Acropora palmata)* can be found in the shallows of Yellowman on Klein Bonaire.

Below Caribbean reef octopus *(Octopus briareus)* are often seen at night on Bonaire's coastal drop-off.

Captain Don's Habitat

The house reef in front of Captain Don's Habitat slopes steeply before dropping off vertically as you swim north from the small jetty in front of the dive shop. Just north of this wall is a sand slope covered in boulder corals and sea rods (*Plexaurella nutans*). Amid these coral branches there are three resident sea horses (*Hippocampus reidi*), which are very difficult to find as they always assume the colour of the corals among which they live. The dive centres all offer 24-hour diving and, around midnight, this reef is excellent with orange ball anemones (*Pseudocorynactis caribbeorum*), lobster, shrimps, hermit crabs, sleeping parrotfish, and even a huge resident tarpon that 'buzzes' you continually on the dive.

Yellowman

Klein Bonaire, known locally as 'Klein', sits in the knuckle of Bonaire, due west, and is only a short 5–10-minute ride across the deep channel that separates the two islands. There are a number of dive sites on Klein Bonaire's northeast side, of which Yellowman is certainly one of the most pristine in the Caribbean. Originally named after a local blond-haired 'Rasta' who sleeps on the beach, many divers prefer to remember the site by the luscious garden of yellow elkhorn and staghorn corals which occur in the shallows. Very few divers ever visit the shallows of Yellowman, preferring the steeply sloping wall with its gigantic tube sponges and thousands of fusiliers, blue chromis and creole wrasse.

TOADFISH AND FROGFISH

Toadfish have got to be some of the most bizarre of the reef inhabitants around the southern and western Caribbean. There are two distinct species and both are found in the shallow waters of Cancún Bay in Mexico all the way across the Caribbean to the north coast of Tobago. They have also been reported from other Central American countries and although they have not been seen in Bonaire, they have been heard, but little else is known of their distribution.

What is most distinctive about these fish comes from their name, 'toadfish'.

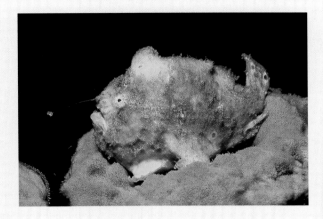

Above Frogfish blend perfectly with their surroundings; only a diver's torch picks out a slight difference in colour.

At night, whilst swimming around the reef, you are actually able to find them by following the sound. Coral reefs are generally quite noisy, but it is most peculiar to hear a distinctive croaking underwater and then to spot a pair of beady eyes watching you from under a coral ledge.

There is no similarity between toadfish and frogfish. Longlure frogfish (*Antennarius multiocellatus*) are anglerfish, relying on superb camouflage to blend in with corals and sponges, and using a lure to attract their prey. This adapted dorsal fin is wiggled about in

They barely resemble their terrestrial counterparts except for one rather astonishing factor – like toads, they make 'croaking' noises which can actually be heard for quite a distance underwater. Living under a coral overhang, they choose an area where the resonance is amplified by the small coral cave.

the water and the motion brings small blennies or gobies within reach of the upward pointing mouth. The pectoral fins have evolved to act like feet, with which it walks around over coral rubble and uses to spring up towards its prey as its mouth opens. A separate species (*Histrio histrio*) is found almost exclusively on sargassum seaweed.

Above Toadfish derive their name from the curious croaking sound they make underwater to attract a mate.

Above The red frogfish in the centre of the photograph resembles the nearby sponge so closely, it is virtually impossible to identify it.

Superior Producer Wreck

The *Superior Producer*, a coastal freighter, rests upright in 32m (107ft) of water. The shallowest part of the wreck, at about 14m (46ft), is the top of the forward mast; the deck and cargo holds are at 22m (72ft). In 1977, the ship was bound for Venezuela from St Anna Baai when she started to take in water just outside the harbour. Already overloaded with a cargo of clothing, liquor, perfume, luggage and other leather goods, she listed and quickly sank. What ensued was a frenzy of looting as the locals dived down to remove her cargo. Many of the islanders had little, or no, diving experience – certainly not in such deep water – and over 70 people apparently needed treatment in the recompression chamber as a direct result of salvaging goods.

The ship is now a classic wreck dive and is considered to be one of the top wrecks in the Caribbean. It is completely festooned in marine life with huge organ-pipe sponges, golden cup corals, sea fans and a multitude of fish. The holds are open and accessible, as are the bridge and accommodation quarters below. Best suited for photography around the rails and open stairwells and the top of the bridge, the wreck is just a little too deep to allow full exploration on one dive; it is fully recommended that a series of dives be undertaken at this exciting and challenging site.

Above The spars across the hold of the *Superior Producer* are festooned in marine life.

Left The stairwell at the bow of the *Superior Producer* is covered in golden cup corals *(Tubastrea coccinea)*.

Beacon Point

Southeast of the Lion's Hotel (a 10-minute boat ride away) is Beacon Point, an exposed headland that is subject to surge conditions on the surface. Underwater, the wall drops away at a 45-degree angle, becoming steeper the further it drops away. Organ-pipe sponges, barrel sponges, sea whips and fan corals stretch out into the current. Parrotfish and bluehead wrasse munch their way along the reef, and almost every coral head has a beaugregory (*Stegastes leucostictus*) in residence, actively protecting its domain and appearing very aggressive. The curious coral formations in the shallows make this site memorable. A huge group of pillar corals (*Dendrogyra cylindrus*) has formed hundreds of individual pillars, all different sizes and unlike the coral's normal growth pattern.

Mushroom Forest

Situated at the most westerly point of Curaçao, Mushroom Forest is 20 minutes by boat from the closest dive centre, All West Diving. The coral heads on the shallow platform reef have been sculpted by tide and weather into mushroom-like forms. The effect is like those fantasy castles that sci-fi artists are so fond of painting. You can weave your way between these coral pillars, all of which have attendant parrotfish, wrasse and schooling blue tangs (*Acanthurus coeruleus*) grazing on the algae that grows around the coral heads. At the end of the dive, you will come across a huge cave cut into the coral platform and extending quite far. Here, far from the light, large boulders are smothered in golden cup coral (*Tubastrea coccinea*).

Right Divers are amazed at the curious formation of the pillar coral forest at Beacon Point in Curaçao.

Tugboat Wreck

The *Tugboat*, or Towboat as it is sometimes called, is about a 20-minute boat ride from the Underwater Curaçao Dive Centre adjacent to the Curaçao Aquarium. Although the journey to the dive site can be rough, the wreck sits upright in only 5m (17ft) of water, just east of three old uprights – the remains of an old pier. The dive boat anchors between two of these uprights, with the wreck lying directly ahead in the shallows. Being small and compact, yet completely overgrown with all manner of corals and sponges, the *Tugboat* is wonderful to dive on and photograph. The wall opposite the wreck drops vertically in some places and here you may find a longsnout sea horse (*Hippocampus reidi*) hanging onto the colourful sponges. This site has a huge number of giant anemones (*Condylactis gigantea*) and every one of them has several different species of attendant shrimps. A large green moray eel *(Gymnothorax funebris)* with a deformed mouth can be found beneath some junk at the stern.

Above Spotted cleaner shrimps *(Periclimenes yucatanicus)* occur on anemones in Curaçao's shallow reefs.

Right The *Tugboat*, located in the shallows of Curaçao, is totally festooned in marine life and is one of the most 'photogenic' wrecks to be visited.

WINDWARD ISLANDS

The southernmost islands in the eastern Caribbean are known collectively as the Windward Islands, and comprise Trinidad, Tobago, Barbados, St Lucia, Grenada, St Vincent and the Grenadines (Bequia, Mustique, Canouan, Mayreau, Tobago Cays, Union, Carriacao, and Ronde), Martinique, Dominica, Guadeloupe, and its satellite Marie Galante. This volcanic chain of islands is lush, tropical, mountainous and incredibly diverse. One of the best diving destinations is Tobago with its spectacular drift dives, manta rays, whale sharks, and the biggest brain corals in the Caribbean. St Lucia has emerged as having one of the highest yields and diversities of all marine species found in the Caribbean, and diving is absolutely superb, particularly at Anse Chastanet.

TRINIDAD AND TOBAGO

Giant Brain Corals and Manta Rays

ROCKY MOUNTAINS AND SAINT GILES ISLANDS · DIVER'S DREAM · *MAVERICK* WRECK ·
BOOKENDS · ANGEL REEF · KELESTON DRAIN

Tobago is always mentioned at the same time as Trinidad, but it is there that the similarity ends. Situated in the far southeast of the Caribbean, these two islands are part of the same republic which gained independence from Britain in 1962. Trinidad and Tobago, 33km (21 miles) apart, were once a continuation of Venezuela at the northeastern flank of South America. Volcanic in origin, but with a mantle of ancient coralline limestone, they are lush and fertile, with both flat agricultural areas and towering hills covered in ancient rainforest. Tobago, in fact, has the oldest protected rainforest in the western hemisphere, first recorded in 1764.

Trinidad is bathed in the nutrient-rich waters that spill out of the Orinoco River and are carried north by the South Equatorial Current, which feeds the Gulf Stream. Unfortunately, this means that the underwater visibility is rather murky, not like the clear water synonymous with the Caribbean. Nevertheless, Trinidad is home to the largest groups of manta rays and whale sharks in the Caribbean, both of which enjoy the nutrient-rich waters.

Throughout the Windward Islands, the majority of diving is done along the more sheltered west coast and it is only in exceptional circumstances that dive operators bother to venture onto the windward side of the islands, even when the weather is perfect. In Tobago, however, the Speyside area on the northeast coast is also sheltered by a small island called Little Tobago and most of the diving actually takes place on the Atlantic side, with absolutely spectacular results.

Created by a volcanic upheaval which raised an ancient coral reef above the waves, Tobago is lush and tropical and appears to be an offshoot of Venezuela with colourful birds, curious insects and diverse forestation. Very mountainous, the main road around the island is a continuous bumpy ride over volcanic ridges and valleys from the Crown Point Airport in the far southwestern tip of the island. There is a short section of dual carriageway outside the capital of Scarborough, but this rapidly gives way to the rugged coast as you travel north to Speyside.

The northerly current passing Trinidad meets a current from South America and here a vortex of tidal streams is created around the offshore volcanic islands causing immensly strong tidal races which can reach over five knots. These can be difficult diving conditions, but under the control of the very experienced dive staff, visiting divers are given the opportunity to 'fly' past submarine cliff walls, pass the largest brain corals in the Caribbean, see sharks, turtles and manta rays and all at breakneck speed, allowing for very long dives with little air consumption because there is so little effort attached to this type of diving.

Best time to go Jan–May, during the dry season when there is least wind. Humidity does cause a problem, though.

Getting there Direct flights from the UK, major European destinations, South America and the USA on most major airlines. Inter-island flights are predominantly run by LIAT and BWIA.

Special interest Visit the rainforests with experienced guides. One of the best snorkelling beaches is at the Arnos Vale Resort, with schools of squid to be found in the shallows.

Accommodation and dive operations Arnos Vale has its own in-house dive resort at the southwest of the island; R and C Divers Den is located on the south coast at Crown Point. At the northern end of the island, Man Friday is located in Charlotteville; Aqua Marine Divers are at the Blue Waters Inn; and Tobago Dive Experience is part of Manta Lodge (in Speyside), which is owned by Sean Robinson. All dives are from open-topped, pirogue-style boats, so protection from the sun is vital.

Electricity supply American-style plugs, 110V.

Emergency information There are recompression chambers at Scarborough General Hospital, Tobago, tel: 639 2551; at St Anne's Fort Garrison, Barbados, tel: (246) 436 6215; and at Hospital de la Meynard, tel: (596) 55 20 00. Divers' Alert Network (DAN), tel: (919) 648 8111.

Previous pages Lush mountains surrounding sheltered bays signify the attraction of the Windward Islands.
Opposite Speyside has a population of Atlantic manta rays *(Manta birostris)* known locally as 'Tobago Taxis'.
Top The pirogue-style dive boat comes very close to shore to enable divers to load their equipment.

Rocky Mountains and Saint Giles Islands

Off the most northerly point of Tobago, the Saint Giles Islands are a rugged group of volcanic, jagged rocks which are vulnerable to the worst storms rolling in from the Atlantic, unhindered by any land mass. More accessible from the small coastal village of Charlotteville, they are about a 10-minute ride by boat from the dive centre. One of the larger satellite rocks has a huge natural arch, known as London Bridge, which offers some magnificent diving along the inner wall. This drops at 45 degrees and is covered in brain corals, boulder corals and sea fans.

Rocky Mountains is a cluster of huge volcanic boulders covered in all manner of marine growth, including brightly coloured sponges, hydroids, featherduster worms and algae. There are massive brain corals, all with attendant cleaning gobies, and all of the same variety.

The sea bed at around 14m (46ft) is a jumble of boulders, corals and sponges, all of which shelter blackbar soldierfish, colourful queen angelfish (*Holacanthus ciliaris*) and countless newly hatched fish fry; there are so many of them, they make the water column appear hazy.

The fry also attract many different predators, including trumpetfish, various jacks, snapper and

grunt. Also commonly to be found among the coral boulders are the larger anemone species (*Condylactis gigantea*), each one playing host to several species of shrimp, in particular *Periclemenes yucatanicus*, which is at the limit of its easterly range here but actually fairly common. Another rather rare find in this area is the big-eyed toadfish, which is much more at home in the western regions; there are several of these fish 'croaking' underwater.

Diver's Dream

Located off the southernmost point of Tobago, this potentially very serious drift dive is totally exhilarating. The dive is a shallow reef plateau approximately 3km (2 miles) south towards Trinidad. Here the might of the current that sweeps along the Atlantic coast is channelled between the two islands at speeds of up to five knots. When entering the water here, divers have to make sure that they form a group together, swim to the sea bed as quickly as possible and use a surface marker buoy to alert the dive boat as to their position.

Here the constant strong current has sculpted the sea bed into long gulleys and overlapping plates of coral limestone. There are thousands of huge barrel sponges, all misshapen and bent over by the strength of the current. As you can imagine, there are also sea fans everywhere; these are aligned perpendicular to the current in order to trap the water-borne nutrients more efficiently. Nurse sharks are commonly seen here, as are lobsters, snapper, grunt, Bermuda chub, and filefish.

Top Blue tangs (*Acanthurus coeruleus*) are usually solitary feeders, picking at algae-covered corals.

Left Trumpetfish (*Aulostomus maculatus*) often hide among coral plumes, waiting for their prey.

Maverick Wreck

The *Maverick*, a 96m (320ft) former ferry, was sunk on 7 April 1997, creating a new dive site on Tobago's southern reefs. This 'roll on, roll off' ferry, which at one time regularly plied the route between Trinidad and Tobago, now rests at a depth of about 31m (103ft). She sits perfectly upright, with her bows pointing due north. The shallowest part of the wreck is 12m (40ft) and all aspects of the ship are completely accessible – divers are able to penetrate the wreck on all levels and on entering the cargo hold in the bow, can exit on the aft deck. Thousands of silversides can be seen above the wreck.

Above The *Maverick* wreck is a newly sunk artificial reef in southwestern Tobago.

Right The deep hold of the *Maverick* is slowly becoming home to a wide array of marine life.

Bookends at Speyside

East of Speyside and south of Little Tobago Island are the Bookends, two distinctive rocks battered by the Atlantic surge. Only in perfect conditions is it possible for divers to negotiate the narrow pass between the rocks. In contrast, when the surge is really strong, the rocks act as a wave barrier and the dive takes place on the wall which runs in a northerly direction towards Little Tobago Island. This is a fairly gentle drift dive, averaging 25m (80ft) to the sloping sea bed, but more generally carried out at around 15m (50ft). The upper portion of the water column above the sloping wall is home to thousands of blue and green chromis, fusiliers, silversides and creole wrasse, all of which are in turn preyed upon by massive tarpon. Large angelfish are everywhere and again, due to the prevailing current, many of the sponges are flattened and fringed with deepwater sea fans.

Angel Reef at Speyside

Goat Island, which is situated between Speyside and Little Tobago Island, is virtually split in two; the gap between the volcanic rocks is straddled by a large house. Angel Reef is the sloping reef wall that tumbles towards the sea bed in majestic form; it consists of huge boulder and brain corals, as well as sea fans, plumes and rods. It is also a drift dive, as most of the dives on the Atlantic side of Tobago are, and it has a profusion of marine life – every known species of Caribbean angelfish appears to congregate in considerable numbers all over the reef. As you make your approach to the northerly end of the island, you will come across two enormous submarine sea mounts blocking your passage. The current will push you over these and, on the far side of the second sea mount, you will see a centuries-old anchor, completely encrusted with sponges and corals.

Left Tobago is home to the largest brain corals in the Caribbean. Several of them are over 4m (14ft) in diameter, such as the one pictured here, easily dwarfing a diver being swept by in the current.

Keleston Drain at Speyside

For sheer exhilaration and also for guaranteed encounters with large animals, Keleston Drain has to be one of the most dramatic dives in the Caribbean. The first part of the dive, known simply as the Drain, is a steeply sloping wall to approximately 15m (50ft). Here the largest brain corals in the Caribbean occur, the record being a specimen over 3.5m (12ft) in diameter. The current here runs from the east to the west until it converges at the southwestern point of Little Tobago where it meets two more currents, creating a vortex of swift-moving water that can toss you around unpredictably and possibly pull you into deeper water.

Zipping past this maelstrom, you cannot even stop and attempt to photograph the nurse sharks which shelter under the boulders. However, turtles, big jacks and southern stingrays (*Dasyatis americana*) seem to be able to swim against the tide effortlessly. Once around the point, the current lessens somewhat as it moves towards the north and you enter a site known as the Cathedral, or more popularly as Manta City.

Little Tobago Island is just one of a very few locations in the world where you can almost guarantee encounters with the Atlantic manta (*Manta birostris*). Although they are not seen on every dive, there have been consistent encounters weekly for over 20 years. It would appear that this area inside Little Tobago Island has such a high concentration of planktonic nutrients that the resident population of around 12 mantas are perfectly happy to stay and feed in this area, allowing divers a chance to swim with one of the most graceful of all the sea's creatures. The mantas approach divers quite readily, seemingly enjoying the human contact, and allowing them to scratch their leathery skin.

Opposite Brilliant red rope sponges *(Amphimedon compressa)* spiral up into the nutrient-rich waters surrounding Tobago.

Right Featherduster worms *(Bispira brunnea)* cluster together amidst a backdrop of colourful sponges, corals and algae.

Best time to go The months of Apr–May are very good – sunny, calm, clear water and overall excellent conditions. The rainy season is from Jun–Nov, which coincides with hurricane season.

Getting there Major international flights from the UK, Europe, Canada, the USA, and South America. One drawback is that the island has two airports: the airport to the north, near the capital of Castries, only handles inter-island traffic, while all international flights are routed through the Hewanorra Airport in the south, making the travelling time to the various resorts somewhat arduous.

Special interest Due to the island's volcanic past and the current volatile future of some of her sister islands, St Lucia has an active interior with its hot springs and sulphur pools. Rainforest tours are another speciality of the island, as well as a visit to the ancient plantation houses.

Dive operation Scuba St Lucia, located on the beachfront at Anse Chastanet.

Electricity supply 220V in British-style three-pin square plugs; American-style 110V adaptors are available from the hotel, or use the shaver two-pin socket.

Emergency information The closest recompression chamber on Barbados is at Dr Mike Brown, tel: (246) 436 6215; Medical Unit Emergencies, tel: (246) 436 5483. Divers' Alert Network (DAN), tel: (919) 648 8111.

ST LUCIA

The Best Shore Reef Dive in the Caribbean

LESLEEN M WRECK • ANSE CHASTANET • THE PINNACLES

St Lucia (pronounced 'Loo-shah') is the second largest of the Windward Islands, located 175km (110 miles) northwest of Barbados and almost equidistant between Martinique in the north and St Vincent in the south. The island was discovered by Christopher Columbus on 13 December 1502 – the Feast of St Lucy – and was therefore named Santa Lucia. Originally owned by the French, who first settled the island in 1650, it became a British dependency in 1814. In 1979, St Lucia gained full independence and became a member of the British Commonwealth.

St Lucia is mountainous and very pretty, with huge banana plantations. The volcanic peaks are topped by Morne Gimie, the highest mountain at 936m (3117ft), but the island is perhaps better known for the Pitons, two peaks created when Mount Soufriere exploded to the south of the town of Soufriere and Anse Chastanet. Dominating the landscape both above and below the water, the peaks are so spectacular that a new local award-winning beer was recently named after them.

The central volcanic ridge is covered in subtropical rainforest and dominates St Lucia. Fast-running streams lead to virtually every bay around the island. The flattest areas are at the northern and southern extremities, but the most interesting are the steep hills virtually smothered in plantations of bananas. You will notice that the banana fruits are covered in blue plastic bags to protect them from the elements until they are ready for picking. Bananas grow in clusters of about 12, which are called 'hands'; a collection of about 10 or so hands is called a 'bunch'.

At Soufriere Bay, the Pitons to the south plunge underwater almost as deep as they are high, with steeply sloping walls covered in sea fans, barrel sponges and low encrusting corals. Not known for its large schools of fish, the overall drama of the area more than makes up for this factor. The sea in this region is never completely clear, and does not have that wonderful 'blue' quality of other Caribbean regions. It is tinged with sulphurous yellow water coming out of underwater vents, similar to those from other islands belonging to this active volcanic group. The sulphur turns the water a greenish colour, but because of the increased temperature associated with the vents, the coral sea fan growths are much more vibrant and diverse.

The marine reserve at Anse Chastanet, just north of Soufriere, is situated inside a sheltered headland, protecting the shallow coastal corals from the worst of the storms. The area is so special that several universities have set up monitoring stations on the reef to research coral growth and species diversity, testimony to the unique nature of the site, in what is often described as the best shore reef dive in the entire Caribbean.

Opposite Queen angelfish *(Holacanthus ciliaris)* generally hide near coral overhangs when danger approaches.
Top Red night shrimps *(Rhynchocinetes rigens)* can often be found off the Anse Chastanet Marine Reserve.

Lesleen M Wreck

Situated about 20 minutes to the north of Anse Chastanet by boat is the wreck of the *Lesleen M.* This 50m (165ft) steel-hulled cargo ship was sunk in 1986 by the Ministry of Fisheries in order to create an artificial reef. Her main mast and wheelhouse were removed as they were deemed a navigational hazard, and the *Lesleen M* now sits upright in about 20m (66ft) of water.

Although the bows and the cargo hold are very interesting and covered in sea fans and sponges, the best area to explore is around the aft part of the ship, where the deck and part of the accommodation quarters can be accessed. The covered aft deck is filled with deep-water gorgonians (*Iciligorgia schrammi*) and the colourful sea rod (*Diodogorgia nodulifera*). The starboard ladders are particularly colourful and a school of blackbar soldierfish (*Myripristis jacobus*) has made its home in the entrance to one of the submerged cabins.

Left The wreck of the *Lesleen M* north of Anse Chastanet is superbly covered in colourful sea fans and is home to thousands of soldierfish.

Above Blackbar soldierfish *(Myripristis jacobus)* form huge social groups on the aft deck, near the stairwell of the shipwreck *Lesleen M*.

Anse Chastanet

The marine reserve in front of the Anse Chastanet Resort, and serviced by Scuba St Lucia, has proved to have the highest yield of marine species in the Caribbean. This small area has so much marine life that you could spend years discovering and describing it all. Accompanied by very experienced dive guides, divers in the small marine nature reserve will come across a shallow platform with sandy gullies between low coral spurs and a near vertical wall in some places that drops to well below a safe diving depth – all this located just a few metres from the shore.

There is a deep cave filled with glassy sweepers (*Pempheris schomburgki*) and near the entrance lives a small red longlure frogfish, although it so closely resembles the small encrusting red sponge (*Spirastrella coccinea*) that it is difficult to detect.

At night, Anse Chastanet also rates as one of the Caribbean's top shore reef dive sites. Each species of Caribbean lobster is present, as well as red night shrimps (*Rhynchocinetes rigens*) and even the rare golden coral shrimp (*Stenopus scutellatus*), which is similar to the banded coral shrimp (*Stenopus hispidus*); interestingly, they are in fact deadly enemies. The sand yields burrowing starfish, rare tube anemones, heart urchins, peacock flounders, and many species of nudibranch and sea hare.

Top The bay at Anse Chastanet in St Lucia has some of the best shore diving in the Windward Islands.

Map of St Lucia showing:
Castries
ST LUCIA
Lesleen M Wreck
Morne Gimie Peak ● 936 m (3117ft)
Anse Chastanet Marine Park
Soufriere
Soufriere Bay
The Pinnacles
Anse Chastanet

The Pinnacles

South of Anse Chastanet, towards the town of Soufriere, is a series of four coral pinnacles with their outer edges on the wall and the inner edges around 15m (50ft). These large coral heads are covered in huge barrel sponges and hundreds of deepwater sea fans. The sheltered areas are brilliantly colourful with all manner of sponges. Large French angelfish (*Pomacanthus paru*) are common and there are also large numbers of juveniles, their vivid yellow-and-black-striped bodies a complete contrast to the adults.

Right Spotted spiny lobsters *(Panulirus guttatus)* are regularly seen on night dives.

Below This banded coral shrimp *(Stenopus hispidus)* clearly shows the egg mass on its underside.

LEEWARD ISLANDS

The Leeward Islands encompass Antigua, Barbuda, St Kitts, Nevis, Sint Maarten/St Martin, St Eustatius, St Barthélémy, Saba, Anguilla, and Montserrat. Throughout the island chain, both the north and south coasts feature areas of often turbulent water, where the might of the Atlantic Ocean meets the Caribbean Sea. Barbuda is said to be the wreck capital of the Leeward Islands,

but there are at present no commercial diving operations on the island to explore the area or to chart and record the shipwrecks.

The islands sit atop a vast submarine mountain ridge, which was above sea level at one time. Between Antigua and Barbuda are the ancient remains of the original land bridge – identical in formation to the sea bed off Cancún.

ANTIGUA AND BARBUDA

A Beach for Every Day of the Year

BIG JOHN · *JETIAS* WRECK · GREEN ISLAND · SUNKEN ROCK

Antigua and Barbuda are located in the middle of the Leeward Islands, 17 degrees north of the Equator, 482km (300 miles) southeast of Puerto Rico and 2093km (1300 miles) southeast of Miami. Separated by about 48km (30 miles) of turbulent water, the two islands are well known for their excellent sailing and diving. Tourism, which to a large extent is centred around the islands' 365 beaches, is the main industry of the area.

Antigua and Barbuda were both already settled by Taino and Arawak Indian tribes at the time Columbus was discovering the other Caribbean islands, and it is debatable whether he even set foot there. He did name one of the islands Santa Maria de la Antigua after a miracle-working saint in the Seville Cathedral. There was no attempt at colonization until 1632, when the British arrived from St Kitts and claimed Antigua. By 1674, sugar cane had been introduced by Sir Christopher Codrington from Barbados. The first plantation, called Betty's Hope, has recently been restored. Based on slave labour, the industry died out when slavery was abolished in 1834, and today the 150 or so mills are mostly in ruin, though some have been converted into homes; all the plantations have reverted to agricultural plots.

Based in sheltered English Harbour, Admiral Horatio Nelson's fleet found no need to return to

the UK, and instead helped stop illegal trade between the USA and the islands. A large percentage of Antigua's population are descendants of these sailors and the plantation slaves. An excellent multimedia presentation above English Harbour depicts the history of the island of Antigua.

Barbuda, the lesser known of the two islands, has over 200 recorded wrecks, yet there are no permanent dive centres on the island. It is generally too far for day boats to travel to Barbuda from Antigua, but there is a superb reef midway between the two islands. Low-lying, scrubby, coralline Barbuda, a 10-minute flight from Antigua, is home to thousands of frigate birds. Settled by Europeans in 1666, the island was used as a stock farm to supply Antigua. The capital, Codrington, is home to a small population of approximately 1500 people. There are steep cliffs on the eastern side of the island, reminiscent of those on Cayman Brac, with large caverns, many containing carved petroglyphs from the original Amerindian settlers.

Today, despite their separateness as two islands, Antigua and Barbuda are one nation, thriving and moving ahead with the times. Internationally recognized as the host for one of the world's top sailing events and boat shows, the islands are incredibly popular due to the hundreds of safe and sheltered anchorages.

Best time to go The rainy months are from Sep–Nov, but you can expect short showers at any time. Average temperature is around 26°C (79°F) with an almost constant trade wind blowing from the east.

Getting there Most visitors arrive by air at VC Bird International Airport, an inter-island hub at the northeast end of Antigua. Most major air carriers from Europe and the USA fly direct to the island and there are daily flights from the eastern Caribbean.

Special interest Devil's Bridge at Indian Town Point is a natural sea-carved cut and arch in the coral limestone shore. English Harbour and Nelson's Dockyard, where Nelson's fleet undertook its refit and hull scraping, has been revitalized with shops, ship's chandleries and small hotels.

Accommodation and dive operations Dive Antigua is based at the Rex Halcyon Cove at Dickenson Bay and is the longest established operation on the island. Long Bay Dive Shop, attached to the Long Bay Hotel, explores the eastern windward side of the main island and the sheltered reefs and bays. Octopus Divers are based at English Harbour on the south coast. Their clients tend to stay in the old dockyard at the Copper and Lumber Store Hotel.

Electricity supply Either American-style 110V two-pin plugs, or British-style 220V square three-pin plug connections.

Emergency information Divers' Alert Network (DAN), tel: (919) 648 8111.

Previous pages English Harbour in Antigua is one of the picturesque natural harbours in the Caribbean.
Opposite Tiger groupers *(Mycteroperca tigris)*, often seen in cleaning stations, are common on offshore reefs.
Top Quiet Long Bay, just one beach off the southeast coast of Antigua, is a favourite for sun worshippers.

Big John

Lying midway between Antigua and Barbuda, Big John (named after John Birk, a large and colourful dive shop owner and conservationist) is a low, ancient coralline, raised sea bed reef reminiscent of the offshore reefs west of Cancún in the Yucatán. Several kilometres long, the exposed offshore reef has a number of sites that have already been explored, and many still to be discovered. Mike's Reef, at a depth of 20m (66ft), boasts a huge population of spiny lobsters (*Panulirus argus*). Divers have encountered groups of over 150 of these creatures, lined up under the low overhanging lip of the ancient coral reef. Nurse sharks (*Ginglymostoma cirratum*) are common, and the Caribbean reef shark (*Carcharhinus perezi*) occasionally occurs.

Large hogfish vie for space amid grouper, moray eels and literally thousands of snapper and grunt. At nearby Lobster Hole, there are rare fingerprint cyphoma (*Cyphoma signatum*) on common sea fans and sea whips, and nurse sharks, southern stingrays (*Dasyatis americana*), Bermuda chubb, sand tile fish and, again, lobster as far as the eye can see. Thankfully this reef is considered too far away by local Antiguan lobster fishermen.

Codrington
BARBUDA

Big John

St John's
ANTIGUA

Above Juvenile blue tangs (*Acanthurus coeruleus*) can develop vertical bars on their bodies at night as camouflage.

Right Arrow crabs (*Stenorhynchus seticornis*) prefer to live under shaded coral overhangs, often in association with anemones.

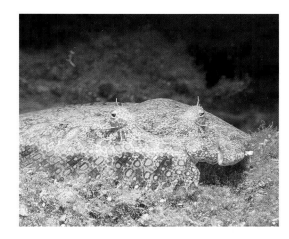

Jetias Wreck

This British freighter, carrying a general cargo of sugar, molasses and rum, foundered and sank off Antigua in 1917. The ship, which operated around the West Indies, was 80m (260ft) long, was driven by a three-cylinder triple expansion steam engine, and had a variable pitch, four-blade propellor. Now lying in only about 7m (24ft) of water, she is liberally encrusted with small soft corals and tiny blue tunicates (*Clavelina picta*), and is also home to hundreds of sergeant majors (*Abudefduf saxatilis*) and a number of small princess parrotfish (*Scarus taeniopterus*).

Green Island

Situated on the southeast coast of Antigua, the leeward side of Green Island has a natural bay where anchorage is easy. Each side of the bay is protected by a fringing reef – boats enter through shallow water and follow the reef to the windward side, where the swell can reduce visibility. There are stands of majestic elkhorn coral (*Acropora*

palmata), as well as some gigantic boulder brain coral (*Colpophyllia natans*). Cleaning gobies (*Gobiosoma genie*) are common on this coral, as are Christmas-tree worms (*Spirobranchus giganteus*). Giant anemones (*Condylactis gigantea*) inhabit the lower depths and small shrimps and diamond-backed blennies can be found nearby.

Above left Peacock flounders *(Bothus lunatus)* are common sand dwellers; their curious flattened shape and moveable eye stalks are quite comical.

Above A lovely Christmas-tree worm *(Spirobranchus giganteus)* is seen here nestled in a colourful group of golden cup corals *(Tubastrea coccinea).*

Sunken Rock

Above the water is a view of British musician Eric Clapton's new home, below is a coralline rock formation the size of a city block that starts at 9m (30ft). A fissure appears and can be followed down to 21m (70ft) before it drops over the wall vertically to 33m (110ft). There are huge coral formations, sponges, sea fans and plumes. Blackbar soldierfish (*Myripristis jacobus*) group together and bigeyes (*Priacanthus arenatus*) play host to cleaning shrimps and gobies. It is interesting that cave-living fish prefer shrimps while open-water reef fish prefer gobies to undertake the picking off of decaying skin and scales.

At the opposite side of Falmouth Bay is Red Rock, where the dive boat's mooring is at 12m (40ft) and the reef slopes beyond 21m (70ft). This largely untouched reef has huge barrel sponges (*Xestospongia muta*), sea fans, brain corals and pink vase sponges (*Niphates digitalis*), while bluehead wrasse (*Thalassoma bifasciatum*) and redband parrotfish (*Sparisoma aurofrenatum*) abound.

Above Rock beauties *(Holacanthus tricolor)* are the most timid of all the Caribbean angelfish.

Left Schools of tiny bluehead wrasse *(Thalassoma bifasciatum)* constantly patrol the reef crests; it is only the males that develop the classic turquoise body and dark blue head.

ST EUSTATIUS AND SABA

Volcanic Pinnacles and Ancient Coralline Reefs

TENT REEF • THE EYE OF THE NEEDLE • DROP-OFF • BARRACUDA REEF

Best time to go See information under Antigua and Barbuda, page 95.

Getting there There are daily flights from Sint Maarten to both Saba and St Eustatius. Saba requires using a DeHavilland STOL (Short Take-Off and Landing). The live-aboard *Caribbean Explorer* also operates around both islands from Sint Maarten.

Special interest The Outer Limits and Eye of the Needle are the tips of volcanic pinnacles thrusting upwards for hundreds of metres and are considered to offer some of the best diving in the eastern Caribbean.

Accommodation and dive operations Dive Statia, the only dive operation in St Eustatius, is located in Lower Town, Oranjestad; the operators are extremely knowledgeable about the island, its reefs and ecosystems. Nearby is Old Gin House, a restored colonial manor house, and the Golden Era Hotel – both are within walking distance of the dive shop. La Maison Sur La Plage offers complete privacy in secluded Zeelandia Bay. There are also numerous apartments for hire. On Saba, there are four dive operators. Sea Saba is one of the most popular and is also allied to some excellent accommodation called Captain's Quarters. Saba Deep Dive Centre and Wilson's Dive Shop are located at Fort Bay.

Emergency information There is a recompression chamber situated in Fort Bay on Saba, attached to the Saba Marine Park. Emergency number only, tel: (011) 599 53295.

First sighted by Christopher Columbus on Sint Maarten Day, 11 November 1493, Saba and St Eustatius form part of the overall group called the Lesser Antilles, which also include the Virgin Islands. The two islands are part of the same volcanic chain as St Kitts, Nevis, Redonda and Montserrat. St Eustatius and Saba lie just north of St Kitts and 35km (28 miles) south of St Martin/Sint Maarten, where air transfer can be arranged. To the east are the much older protrusions of Antigua and Barbuda. Dominated by its volcanic past, the tiny island of Saba, in particular, rises vertically for 900m (2989ft). Its breathtaking steep sides run down to the water's edge, creating some exciting offshore diving on submarine peaks and walls. Known as the 'Queen of the Caribbean Sea', Saba (pronounced 'Say-bah') is capped by the aptly named Mount Scenery and is actually the smallest of the Dutch Antilles (which also include Curaçao, Bonaire, Aruba, St Barthélémy and Sint Maarten).

There are no beaches on Saba; the populace clings tenaciously to the sides of the mountain, and the island's Juancho Yrausquin Airport has to be seen to be believed. At only 360m (1200ft), it has the shortest commercial runway in the world and is as close as you want to get to the cliffs (a bit like landing on the deck of an aircraft carrier). The capital, known as The Bottom, sits above Fort Bay, which is the only protected harbour on the island.

The volcanic activity which gave rise to Saba also formed other subterranean peaks that failed to reach the surface. These offshore pinnacles are approximately 30m (100ft) deep and they are a natural oasis for marine life, attracting several schools of fish that play around the sponges and the delicate corals.

St Eustatius was formerly one of the main trading centres of the Caribbean. Statia, as it is referred to by the locals, is topped by a peak at either end. The largest formation at the south of the island, known as The Quill, has a huge crater, the interior of which is covered with tropical rainforest and traversed by several nature trails. Similarly with St Kitts, there are no long, golden beaches here – only black volcanic sand for the tourists to lie on.

Without a single shot being fired, St Eustatius was taken by Admiral George Rodney in 1781, in retaliation to the islanders being the first to recognize the independence of the United States.

It is only now, with tourism being the primary industry, that Statia is better equipped to support its 2000 local inhabitants. The capital, Oranjestad, is split into two distinct areas: Upper Town, on the hill above Gallows Bay, and Lower Town next to the sea. The restored Fort Orange, complete with stockade, is situated in Upper Town, while Lower Town features a variety of accommodation as well as Dive Statia, the only operator on the island.

Opposite Popular St Barthélémy in the French West Indies is known for its scenery and superb beaches.
Top Blackbar soldierfish *(Myripristis jacobus)* often form large groups under ancient coralline overhangs.

Tent Reef

A short boat ride west of Fort Bay, opposite Tent Bay, is Tent Reef, probably the most popular shallow reef dive on Saba. The reef is a large coralline rocky ledge that runs parallel to the shoreline. In many places it is undercut and large caves and tunnels have formed, which are quite safe to swim through. This is an incredibly colourful site with red, yellow and pink sponges interspersed with beautiful golden cup corals (*Tubastrea coccinea*). When it is overcast, they extend their polyps into the current and at night they filter-feed on passing planktonic particles. The huge boulders in the shallower water are excellent for macrophotography.

Left Slender filefish *(Monacanthus tuckeri)* tend to hide amidst coral sea fans and rope sponges; this makes them much harder to spot.

Below Many species of shrimp hide in tube sponges during the daylight hours and only emerge from the safety of the sponges at night.

Below Wherever you find sponges, you will find fish using them – not just for protection, but also as a place to lie in wait for unwary prey.

Below Sharpnose pufferfish *(Canthigaster rostrata)* generally prefer to rest within the embrace of sponges during the night.

The Eye of the Needle

This dive is part of a site called The Third Encounter, 1.5km (1 mile) west of Ladder Bay. It comprises a series of pinnacles, all rising from a connective sea mount. Each pinnacle has a name, and all of these dives are regarded as fairly serious undertakings and are for experienced divers only.

Eye of the Needle is a vertical protrusion rising from 75m (250ft) to 27m (90ft) and is only 15m (50ft) in diameter. A profusion of huge, orange, elephant's ear sponges (*Agelas clathrodes*), deep-water sea fans (*Iciligorgia schrammi*) and sea whips (*Ellisella elongata*) exists. Sheet coral (*Agaricia grahamae*) cascades into the depths and above all of this growth is a moving column of creole wrasse (*Clepticus parrai*). Nurse sharks are often spotted resting on the ledges and turtles regularly swim past.

Above The impressive elephant's ear sponge (*Agelas clathrodes*) occurs commonly around Saba.

Left This pinnacle of Eye of the Needle is located at 300 degrees from the dive boat mooring buoy.

Below Sea rods and plumes, moving in the current, provide shelter for many species of small fish.

Venom is generally used for defensive purposes. You soon learn that if the creature you are approaching does not swim away, it must have some form of defence. These creatures include small coelenterates and jellyfish, and the defences range from the tiny bristles of fireworms to the modified fin spines of various fish, anemones, sea urchins, starfish, molluscs and corals. In general, stinging mechanisms around the mouth are for offensive purposes and stinging parts along the back and tail are defensive.

aim is paralysis rather than ingestion. Most jellyfish sting, but few are dangerous. The Portuguese man-of-war occurs in the Caribbean. It is highly toxic and exposure to its stinging cells may require hospital treatment.

Sea wasps (*Carybdea alata*) can be seen in shallow warm water at night. Their stings can be quite severe, causing nausea, muscle cramps and even breathing difficulties. They should always be avoided, but take particular attention during night dives as they swarm near the surface, wherever a light shines.

on its stem, each 'berry' armed with nematocysts. *Corallimorphan* covers large areas of dead coralline limestone boulders on the northern Caribbean reefs. If disturbed, these creatures produce sticky white filaments filled with nematocysts.

Hydroids, such as the stinging hydroid (*Aglaophynia latecarinata*), have featherlike plumes which can inflict a rather nasty sting on the softer areas of your skin if you brush up against them. The most common stinger in this vast family is fire coral (see page 118).

Above The spotted scorpionfish *(Scorpaena plumieri)* is commonly found in shallow water.

Above Fireworms *(Hermodice carunculata)* have tufts of hair growing along their bodies.

Above Long-spined sea urchins *(Diadema antillarium)* can inflict rather serious wounds.

Different creatures have different toxins. Most cause numbness, irritation or paralysis, while some kill nerves or blood cells, attack muscles and affect internal organs. Most have a cumulative effect and some even cause death in humans. About 50 deaths each year are attributed to sea stings of some nature.

The most common stinger is the jellyfish, particularly in tropical oceans where the Portuguese man-of-war (*Physalia physalis*) and the box jellyfish are prevalent. Jellyfish are all members of the same superfamily which includes corals and anemones. Their (primarily offensive) stinging mechanism is a hooked barb fired by a coiled hydraulic spring. These barbs, or nematocysts, are held inside a trap-door until released by touch or by chemicals in the water. The hollow barbs are filled with toxins which are released as the stinger penetrates its victim. The primary

Where thimble jellyfish (*Linuche unguiculata*) occur, there is a chance that smaller, almost invisible, micro-organisms could be present in the water; wear a full wetsuit with a protective hood and gloves or the new style of Lycra skin suit. If you are stung, you may have to resort to hydro-cortisone cream. Other local remedies are available for stings, but acetic acid (vinegar) is in fact as good as anything. In cases of severe stinging, however, medical attention will be required.

Anemones, hydroids and corals are closely related and all have harmful representatives. Most anemones will not do any harm to the relatively thick skin on your fingers, but many can inflict rather painful 'burns' on the softer parts on the inside of your arms or legs. The berried anemone (*Alicia mirabilis*), found in Bermuda, throughout the Caribbean, the Red Sea and the Indo-Pacific, has warty tubercles

Even the most innocuous-looking creatures often have a hidden battery of stingers. A few vase sponges have tiny calcium spicules that when rubbed can cause severe irritation, rashes and sores. Fireworms (*Hermodice carunculata*) have clumps of white hairs which display bristles when touched. These bristles break off in the skin, causing burning and intense irritation. Though not deadly, it needs treatment – use hot water and vinegar.

Members of the stonefish and scorpionfish families are often associated with lethal stings. Because they look just like pieces of coral rubble, a misplaced foot is generally the cause of the incident. True stonefish are not found in the Caribbean, but a variety of scorpionfish are. These are not considered dangerous, but avoid the spines of their dorsal fins. If you are stung, quickly place the affected area into very hot water.

Other marine stingers are, of course, the stingrays. If you are 'communicating' with a stingray, never grab hold of its tail or sit on its back, as the tail holds the stinging mechanism. The stingray may spring it forward in a reflex action, thus erecting the spine and causing serious damage.

Not all stingers are large and obvious. Nudibranchs eat stinging hydroids, and anemones can store the nematocysts of their prey in their own tentacles. When attacked, they use the stored nematocysts in defence. Cone shells may inflict lethal jabs into unwary shell collectors.

Above The Portuguese man-of-war *(Physalia physalis)* may have tentacles 9m (30ft) long.

Sea urchins and starfish seem to lie in wait for unwary humans. The spines of sea urchins can be poisonous; even if not, they will pierce the skin – even through gloves – and leave painful wounds. The long-spined sea urchin *(Diadema antillarum)* should be avoided as the spines are quite brittle and can easily break off in the flesh. Made of calcium, they should dissolve after a few days, but deeply embedded spines could leave permanent scarring and patients may have to be treated for shock.

If a creature does not retreat, exhibits bright colours or takes a defensive posture, it probably has a defence mechanism. In order to avoid any painful inflictions, never dive in just a swimming costume – wear a full wetsuit or Lycra suit. Be cautious, and try to gain an understanding of these much maligned stingers of the sea.

Drop-Off

Located off the south coast of Statia, opposite Buccaneer Bay, Drop-Off is part of a huge, ancient spur-and-groove reef system which follows the contour of the sea bed all the way to St Kitts. The sand plain above the reef is at about 18m (60ft) and the reef drops down to over 45m (150ft). Most people tend to dive over the reef to greater depths where there are deep-water gorgonian sea fans, sheet corals, boulder and brain corals. Long sea whips spiral up to the light and creole wrasse are everywhere. The sand plain has stingrays, sand tile fish and yellowhead jawfish *(Opistognathus aurifrons)*. Atlantic spadefish *(Chaetodipterus faber)* cruise into the area in small hunting packs and there are always barracuda *(Sphyraena barracuda)* to be spotted.

Barracuda Reef

Nearby Kay Bay is a large coralline ledge, a mere remnant of an ancient fringing reef with numerous underhangs, caverns and caves. A host of spiny lobsters *(Panulirus argus)* are to be found here, as well as banded coral shrimps *(Stenopus hispidus)* and also arrow crabs *(Stenorhynchus seticornis)*. Hermit crabs are quite common in the area, and can often be seen, dragging their mobile homes behind them. The best exploring depth is around 15–21m (50–70ft) where an old anchor lies, which serves as a guide for returning to your entry point. There are also several large pipe sponges, barrel sponges, gorgonian sea fans and sea whips here. Fish life includes rock beauties *(Holacanthus tricolor)*, white-spotted filefish *(Cantherhines macroceros)*, smooth trunkfish *(Lactophrys triqueter)*, and balloonfish *(Diodon holocanthus)*.

Zeelandia Bay

ST EUSTATIUS

Oranjestad · The Quill

Kay Bay
Barracuda Reef Drop-off

Above Peacock flounders *(Bothus lunatus)* raise their pectoral fin as a sign of aggression.

Left Sand divers *(Synodus intermedius)* lie in wait under coral overhangs and sponges for unwary prey.

105

ST KITTS AND NEVIS

Old-Style Colonialism

NAG'S HEAD • SANDY POINT • *RIVER TOIRE* WRECK • MONKEY SHOAL • THE VENTS • DEVIL'S CAVES

St Christopher's, known as 'the Mother Colony' because it is the seat of administration, or St Kitts as it is affectionately known, was discovered in 1493 and named after Christopher Columbus who first landed near the site of Old Road Bay on the Caribbean side of the island. Some of the earliest settlement remains are still to be seen along this stretch of coastline, and near the village of Trinity there are carved motifs from the first indigenous islanders, the Carib and Arawak Indians, who called the island *Liamuiga*, meaning 'the fertile land'. Shaped like a frying pan, the island is 37km (23 miles) long and just over 10km (6 miles) wide. It has a volcanic interior with two massive peaks, featured as stars on the national flag; the highest is Mount Liamuiga at 1000m (3792ft).

Because of their volcanic origin, the northern beaches of St Kitts are covered in black sand. The underwater terrain is very similar in topography to the Virgin Islands. The only reasonable beaches are situated in the extreme south of the island, but even then they are 'dirty' in colour. Being volcanic, the island is incredibly fertile and every inch of agricultural land is taken up by sugar cane, which is harvested from January to July by an immigrant work force from Guyana.

To the north of the island near the village of Tabernacle, facing the Atlantic, is an area known as Black Rocks where the sea has pounded the shore over the centuries and eroded the hard volcanic rock and ancient ironstone reef into curious shapes. Several offshore reefs act as a barrier to stormy seas, yet the coast has claimed its share of ships, including a new, small coastal trader which sits high and dry above the tumultuous waves.

Across the southern channel lies St Kitts' sister island, Nevis. It is a 45-minute ride by daily ferry from Basseterre, capital of St Kitts, to Nevis's capital, Charlestown, nestled at the foot of a huge dormant volcano. Unlike St Kitts, Nevis does have golden coral sand beaches in the north and west, and is virtually round in shape with a diameter of 11km (7 miles).

Similarly with St Kitts, a sugar-cane industry used to dominate the island's economy; today there are only market gardens and thousands of wild coconut palms. Guided walks through the rainforest are an attraction, as well as tours of interestingly rebuilt former sugar plantation buildings and mills. The Horatio Nelson Museum features the largest collection of Admiral Lord Nelson's memorabilia. Fort Charles was a stronghold during the 17th century, but fell into disrepair after the Treaty of Paris in 1814.

There are several interesting wrecks around these islands, including the *Christena*, which capsized in 1970 with the loss of over two hundred lives. Due to political pressure, and out of respect for the dead, no diving is allowed on this ship.

Best time to go See information under Antigua and Barbuda, page 95.

Climate The islands are in the path of the northeast trade winds and the climate is equable. There is a steady breeze year-round and the humidity is low. The water temperature is chilly from Nov–May and full wetsuits are therefore recommended.

Getting there Fly direct from the UK by BWIA (via Antigua), or via Miami, Puerto Rico or Paris (Air France to Sint Maarten and then a transfer). Inter-island connections are operated by LIAT, WINAIR and American Eagle.

Special interest Visit the subterranean hot water vents off Nevis. Near the wreck of the *Talata*, sulphur tinges the water green. There are no conservation areas in the region – the first is being planned at Sandy Point, northwest of the island. Meanwhile tourists may recover shells. This should, however, be discouraged as dead shells act as nesting areas for fish and homes for hermit crabs.

Accommodation and dive operations In St Kitts, Pro Divers in Turtle Bay are allied to Horizons Villas Resort; Kenneth's Dive Shop has a custom-built platform dive boat. Scuba Safaris, with Oualie Beach Resort, is in Nevis. For great food, try Nisbet Plantation Hotel and the Old Manor House on Nevis, and Horizons Villas Resort on St Kitts.

Emergency information Closest recompression chamber is on Saba. Divers' Alert Network (DAN), tel: (919) 648 8111.

Opposite Wrecked by a hurricane, the *River Toire* off the east coast of St Kitts is popular among divers.
Top The sheltered bay of Basseterre is where the cruise ships drop anchor when visiting the islands.

Nag's Head

Nag's Head, close to the southernmost point of St Kitts, is primarily volcanic in origin, with a tumble of boulders lying at the bottom of a scree slope which extends for 15m (50ft) underwater. From here a sloping sand plain takes you to a mini wall, which drops down another 9m (30ft). The best part of the dive is undoubtedly to be found in the vicinity of the boulder slope where there are thousands of assorted nooks and crannies harbouring all manner of marine life. On the sand plain, for instance, there are large numbers of damselfish, lizardfish and longsnout butterflyfish (*Chaetodon aculeatus*). Small sea fans have their attendant flamingo tongues (*Cyphoma gibbosum*) and fireworms (*Hermodice carunculata*) are quite common, their good looks masked by the thousands of tiny hairlike barbs which can easily penetrate your skin.

Sandy Point

To the northwest of St Kitts, opposite the village of Sandy Bay, is a convoluted spur-and-groove reef which drops down to 20m (66ft). At a depth of 12m (40ft), there are two huge old admiralty anchors, now heavily encrusted in coral. In the shallows you will find garden eels (*Heteroconger halis*) and peacock flounders (*Bothus lunatus*). This site is also known for helmet gurnards (*Dactylopterus volitans*). Large barrel sponges are common, as are many of the much smaller encrusting sponges and algae. The reef offers large numbers of snapper and grunt, and good quality corals and sponges, and has been earmarked as a future conservation zone.

Below The anchor in this reef has now become home to abundant quantities of marine life.

Above Basseterre, the capital of St Kitts, is located on the sheltered west coast of the island.

Black Rocks
Tabernacle
Mount Liamuiga
1000m (3792ft)
Sandy Point
ST KITTS
Old Road Bay
Basseterre
River Toire Wreck
Frigate Bay
Nag's Head

River Toire Wreck

The *River Toire* (pronounced 'Taw'), a former coastal cargo ship that used to ply the waters of the Leeward Islands, was anchored off Frigate Bay when she was caught in a hurricane and quickly sank. In subsequent storms she was split in two and in 1995 the aft section was turned around. The wreck is home to the largest number of bristle worms, or fireworms (*Hermodice carunculata*), you have ever seen. The superstructure is covered in sea plumes, sea fans, small encrusting sponges, Christmas-tree worms (*Spirobranchus giganteus*) and large areas of sargassum seaweed. If you look between the seaweed you may be very fortunate to find the sargassum filefish and the sargassum frogfish (*Histrio histrio*). At the bottom of a collapsed crane there is an anemone with attendant cleaner shrimps (*Periclimenes pedersoni*). Spiny lobsters can be found under the bows and there are several pairs of French angelfish (*Pomacanthus paru*). You can swim down the

Above During night dives, turtles should not be disturbed as they rest amidst the corals and sponges.

stern companionway, which is now encrusted in various soft and hard corals, and see several schools of blackbar soldierfish. At night, the deck and funnel are alive with roving hermit crabs, arrow crabs and red night shrimps. Pufferfish rest in the sponges which become translucent pink, orange and yellow by torchlight.

Below The bridled burrfish (*Chilomycterus antennatus*) can inflate itself like a pufferfish.

Below The spotted drum (*Equetus punctatus*) only shows its spots on reaching maturity.

Below Christmas-tree worms (*Spirobranchus giganteus*) are the most common Caribbean tube worms.

Monkey Shoal

Monkey Shoal, a huge submarine atoll that never quite made it to the surface, is located midway between St Kitts and Nevis and is visited by dive centres from both islands. The trip to the site is around 30 minutes, and it can be fairly choppy on the surface. The average depth is 12m (40ft) at the inner sand patch, but the outside wall drops

Above Slender filefish *(Monacanthus tuckeri)* are often found hiding among the fronds of sea plumes.

Left Smooth trunkfish *(Lactophrys triqueter)* are triangular in shape and move in short bursts of speed.

The Vents

At a depth of 30m (100ft), amid a group of large coral outcrops, there are several large geothermal vents which are distinguished by the surrounding rocks having a mustard-brown coloration and by a constant stream of heated fresh water from the volcanic depths. This creates a phenomenon called a halocline, where a shimmering effect is caused by a mix of waters of different temperatures and salinity. Although difficult to find, the largest of the vents often has a small shoal of silverside minnows. Bits of algal debris also come up through the vents and all of the surrounding area features hundreds of strands of whip corals as well as perfect black coral bushes, which are quite rare in some parts of the Caribbean.

Devil's Caves

Off the southwest coast of Nevis in 12m (40ft) of water are numerous caves, caverns, swim-throughs and canyons, all topped by a flat fringing reef consisting of small sea fans, sea whips and boulder corals. Fire coral is also prevalent and should be avoided as the tiny 'hairs' on the tips of the coral are barbed, easily penetrating the skin and causing a burning irritation. At the entrance to the largest of the tunnels, the 'flukes' of a huge admiralty anchor can still be discerned, covered in marine life and embedded into the reef.

The tunnels are home to shoals of glasseye snappers (*Heteropriacanthus cruenatus*), blackbar soldierfish (*Myripristis jacobus*) and glassy sweepers (*Pempheris schomburgki*). Numerous cleaning stations can be seen, turtles are common and some of the deeper caves also have nurse sharks. This is an excellent dive in shallow water and should not be missed.

Above The minute juvenile smooth trunkfish is only about the size of a pea, and its tiny little fins can barely manage to propel it.

Below Honeycomb cowfish (*Lactophrys polygonia*) are quite common around the shallow caverns to the southwest of Nevis.

to well beyond safe diving depths. This reef is so vast – over 3km² (2 square miles) – that there are literally hundreds of dives to explore.

Highlights include the Finger, a giant spur-and-groove formation that stretches well out into deep water with superb corals and a resident school of Atlantic spadefish (*Chaetodipterus faber*); The Ledges, a huge series of ledges with thin fingerlike projections under which large schools of blackbar soldierfish (*Myripristes jacobus*) can be found; and The Donut which, as its name suggests, is a large circular sandy formation comprising an 'O' of small corals and sponges in the centre and an outer 'ring' of corals. Spiny lobsters (*Panulirus argus*) are common, as are arrow crabs (*Stenorhynchus seticornis*).

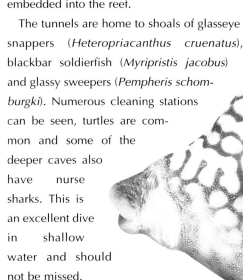

VIRGIN ISLANDS

When Christopher Columbus first discovered these islands strewn across the ocean during his second exploration of the West Indies in 1493, there were so many of them, and of such unspoiled beauty, that he collectively named them 'Los Once Mil Virgines', after St Ursula and her 11,000 virgin followers. The islands are located some 95km (60 miles) to the east of Puerto Rico and about 1800km (1100 miles) to the southeast of Miami. Primarily known for their safe anchorages in a multitude of secluded bays and inlets, the Virgin Islands are split into two distinct and entirely separate areas – to the north are the British Virgin Islands (a British crown colony), and to the south the US Virgin Islands, an unincorporated territory of the USA.

BRITISH VIRGIN ISLANDS

Gigantic Granite Boulders and Rocky Pinnacles

THE INDIANS • RMS *RHONE* WRECK • *CHIKUZEN* WRECK • THE INVISIBLES

The Virgin Islands are the remains of a huge subterranean mountain plateau that erupted millennia ago. There are some 50 islands and cays (pronounced 'keys') clustered around the Sir Francis Drake Channel. Named after the English explorer who sailed through the islands in 1585 en route to Hispaniola (now the Dominican Republic), the channel separates the island chain and is the connecting waterway between the Atlantic Ocean and the Caribbean Sea.

Besides Sir Francis Drake, notorious pirates settled on the islands, including Henry Morgan, Sir John Hawkins and Blackbeard, possibly the most infamous of all, who was reputed to have put 15 mutiny-minded men ashore on the island of Dead Chest (a small scrubby isle between Salt and Peter islands to the south of Road Town), with only a 'yo-ho-ho and a bottle of rum' between them!

Tortola Island is 19km (12 miles) long and 5km (3 miles) at its widest part. Volcanic in origin with high moutain peaks, the Ridge Road traversing it is not only breathtaking but can be nerve-wracking due to the dramatic topography. Virgin Gorda is about half the size of Tortola. Situated to the northeast, it can be reached by small plane or by a regular 30-minute ferry service. The island's pace of life and ambience is totally different from Tortola – here you can truly relax and enjoy some

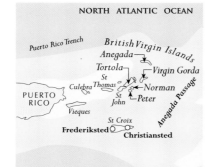

NORTH ATLANTIC OCEAN

Puerto Rico Trench

British Virgin Islands
Anegada
Tortola
St Virgin Gorda
Culebra Thomas
St John Norman
Peter

PUERTO RICO

Vieques

St Croix
Frederiksted
Christiansted

Anegada Passage

of the best diving in the eastern Caribbean. As a bonus there is a chance of sighting humpback whales (*Megaptera nodosa*) during the spring.

South of the Sir Francis Drake Channel lie the islands of Ginger, Cooper, Salt (where the wreck of the *Rhone* is situated), Dead Chest, Peter, and Norman, with many rocky pinnacles, islets and cays in between. North of Tortola lie Jost Van Dyke, Guana Island, Great Camanoe, the Dogs (named after the barking sound made by a now extinct population of Caribbean seals), Mosquito Island, Eustatia, Necker Island (owned by Richard Branson), and Beef Island where the international airport is situated. Anegada, which lies 40km (25 miles) northeast of Tortola, has the largest barrier reef in the eastern Caribbean (the third largest in the world); the island is credited with over 300 shipwrecks.

The National Parks Board has been installing mooring buoys since 1989, and there are now over 180 out of a possible target of 250. However, it is uncertain whether these additional moorings will be needed, due to the level of diving done by only a few operators around the existing locations, which means there is no overlap or congestion at the best dive sites. The mooring buoys have completely eliminated anchor damage, and sites which had previously been rather badly damaged are now fully recovered.

Best time to go See information under US Virgin Islands, page 120.

Getting there Flights from London's Gatwick are serviced by Caledonian and operated by British Airways, but due to the size of the international airport on Beef Island, they are first routed through San Juan in Puerto Rico, with a link by American Eagle.

Special interest Hire a small skiff at the Bitter End Yacht Club on Virgin Gorda and go out to Saba Rock, home of the legendary wreck hunter and latter-day pirate, Bert Kilbride. The Prospect Reef Hotel on Tortola has an eco-friendly holiday package for children. The Baths on Virgin Gorda are a spectacular clump of gigantic granite boulders that tumble into the sea amid tall palm trees and a gorgeous beach.

Accommodation and dive operations
Kilbrides Underwater Tours at the Bitter End Yacht Club on Virgin Gorda is ideal for all the northern sites and Anegada. Dive BVI on Virgin Gorda work from Leverick Bay. At Prospect Reef Resort, west of Road Town on Tortola, Baskin In The Sun is based at the small marina. The next port of call is Nanny Cay where Blue Water Divers are based. Underwater Safaris are allied to the Treasure Isle Hotel in the main marina of Road Town. The superb live-aboard dive boat *Cuan Law*, operated by the Trimarine Boat Co. Ltd out of Tortola, is the only way you can truly appreciate the islands.

Emergency information See information under US Virgin Islands, page 120.

Previous pages Sunset at Bitter End Yacht Club on Virgin Gorda in the British Virgin Islands is spectacular.
Opposite The massive granite blocks on the beach at Virgin Gorda are known the world over as 'The Baths'.
Top Sharpnose pufferfish (*Canthigaster rostrata*) can be found around sponges where they seek shelter.

Above The undersides of the coral reefs in the Virgin Islands are a mass of colourful organisms, so remember always to use torchlight when diving.

Opposite The Invisibles, near Necker Island, are huge granite boulders festooned in golden cup corals and are home to schools of snapper and grunt.

FIRE CORAL

Fire coral (*Millepora alcicornis*), though itself not a true coral, is a member of the Cnidarian phylum which includes true corals, anemones and jellyfish. Always found in shallow waters, the two species occurring in the Caribbean tend to cover shipwrecks as well as dead corals and sea fans. Wherever any coral has been damaged, fire coral is one of the first colonizers. It is creamy orange in colour and has white tips. Closer inspection of these tips will reveal that they are covered in thousands of tiny hairs, each consisting of a battery of stinging cells or nematocysts which can cause a painful irritation on the softer parts of your skin; this can turn septic. Fire coral, a member of the hydroid family, should be avoided.

Top Branching fire coral (*Millepora alcicornis*) shows its barbed nematocysts.

Below Blade fire coral (*Millepora complanata*) is also armed with stinging cells.

The Indians

Near Pelican Island (a satellite of Norman Island), there are four rocky outcrops which resemble an Indian's headdress from a distance. The outcrops, volcanic in origin, have sheer walls cut by ledges and connected by small swim-throughs and tunnels. Coral-encrusting species to be found here are sea plumes (*Pseudopterogorgia* sp.) and giant sea rods (*Plexaurella nutans*). The stony corals are mainly low and encrusting and consist of several species of brain coral and star coral. In the shallower areas, fire corals (*Millepora alcicornis* and *Millepora complanata*) predominate. There are always fairly large schools of snapper and grunt, and small shifting shoals of silverside minnows can also be seen in the caves. Trumpetfish (*Aulostomus maculatus*) and pufferfish (*Canthigaster rostrata*) are quite common, as well as several species of butterflyfish and angelfish.

Nearby The Indians, on the extreme eastern end of Norman Island, is Angelfish Reef. The island shelves steeply away and is literally a garden of soft corals, huge barrel sponges and sea fans. As the name implies, there are also quite a large number of angelfish, the four most common species being the queen angelfish, grey angelfish, French angelfish and rock beauty.

RMS Rhone Wreck

Now regarded as one of the top 10 wrecks in the world, the Royal Mail Steamer (RMS) *Rhone*, and the area surrounding it, has been declared a national marine park, the first of its kind in the British Virgin Islands. The wreck is well-known for its starring role in Peter Benchley's film, *The Deep*, and it is probably one of the most dived wrecks in the entire Caribbean.

Launched on 11 February 1865, the RMS *Rhone* was acknowledged to be one of the very best steel-hulled transatlantic ships of her time. At a length of 95m (310ft), a width of 12m (40ft) and weighing 2738 gross registered tons, she was able to carry a total of 253 first-class passengers, 30 in second class and 30 in third class. There were only 18 passengers plus a crew of 129 on board the RMS *Rhone* when she was swept to destruction on 29 October 1867 in the worst hurricane ever to have hit the Virgin Islands.

The *Rhone* foundered on Salt Island, split her hull and took with her all but one passenger and 21 crew members. The wreck now lies in two

Above The Indians are a group of distinctive rocks to the southwest of the British Virgin Islands.

distinct parts from 6–27m (20–90ft). The forward part of the hull and bowsprit are in the deepest water and are completely open. You can swim right through the ribs of the ship, surrounded by numerous schools of snapper and squirrelfish. The dive guides take great delight in showing you the one remaining intact porthole, as, sadly, the wreck has been badly plundered over the years. Despite the area's marine national park status, every so often someone is arrested for removing *Rhone* artefacts from the site. The punishment for anyone found illegally interfering with the wreck is deportation.

The stern of the ship, still with her four-blade propellor embedded in the reef, is open and you can swim along the propellor shaft to the gear box and boilers, which are now home to squirrelfish, snappers, banded coral shrimps, and encrusting and brightly coloured corals. Filefish and grouper, parrotfish and angelfish vie for your attention.

Chikuzen Wreck

Located to the south of Anegada, and about 15km (9½ miles) northwest of Virgin Gorda, is reputedly the second-largest barrier reef in the Caribbean. It is also the resting place of the *Chikuzen* wreck, a former Japanese refrigerator ship used in the long-line fishing trade and later as a warehouse in St Martin. She was taken to sea to be sunk, but currents carried her 113km (70 miles) from St Martin to the British Virgin Islands before she eventually sank in September 1981 in 23m (75ft) of water. At 74m (246ft) long, and resting on her port side, she is home to an array of pelagic marine life, including snapper, grunt and jacks. Large schools of barracuda await you as you drop from the surface, and the entangled rigging lines are covered in sponges and soft corals. The shape of the decks has been transformed by the profuse coral and sponge growth.

The Invisibles

The Invisibles are located due east of Necker Island and comprise a jumble of huge granite blocks, sculpted by wave action. Two of the pinnacles, the tops of which are smothered in fire coral (*Millepora alcicornis*), lie just beneath the surface. These granite boulders have created swim-throughs, small gulleys, caves and dramatic archways, all adorned with lovely colourful sponges and encrusting soft and hard corals. The undersides of the boulders are thickly covered in golden cup-corals (*Tubastrea coccinea*) and red encrusting sponges (*Diplastrella megastellata*), and they are also surrounded by blackbar soldier-fish (*Myripristis jacobus*), glasseye snapper (*Heteropriacanthus cruenatus*) and squirrelfish (*Holocentrus adscensionis*).

To the north of the boulders, the corals flatten out somewhat until you reach a sand plain where sand tile fish and flounders can be seen. A challenging swim above this sand plain yields encounters with Atlantic spadefish (*Chaetodipterus faber*), which are similar to the batfish in the Indo-Pacific region. Sharks are a regular occurrence too.

Inshore from the Invisibles is a shallow reef protecting Oil Nut Bay. Bottoming out at 15m (50ft) on the sand of the outer edge, spotted eagle rays and southern stingrays are often seen. In the shallower areas of the reef, huge sea plumes drape themselves over pristine corals and large lobsters wander around. This is a superb site for macrophotography, as there are thousands of Christmas-tree worms (*Spirobranchus giganteus*) as well as schools of snapper and grunt.

Above right Schools of snapper and grunt can often be found in the interior of wrecks.

Centre right The *Rhone's* propeller, embedded in the reef, is now overgrown with marine life.

Bottom right The ribs and spars of shipwrecks make a perfect backdrop for marine photography.

Anegada Island

Chikuzen Wreck

BRITISH VIRGIN ISLANDS

Necker Island The Invisibles

Eustatia Island
Oil Nut Bay

Virgin Gorda Island

US VIRGIN ISLANDS

The American Paradise

THE TUNNELS • THE YELLOW BRICK ROAD • *WITSHOAL* WRECK • FRENCHCAP CAY • CANE BAY

Best time to go The climate is equable throughout the year. There is a hurricane risk from Sep–Jan, but only very rarely may this affect your holiday. Summers are hot and humid with temperatures rising to 40°C (90°F), so take care not to overexpose yourself to the sun, particularly when on dive boats. A high factor waterproof sunscreen should be worn at all times, as well as a hat.

Getting there There are regular serviced flights from all of the major American airports such as Miami, Houston and Chicago, straight into St Croix and St Thomas.

Special interest Visit the Steeple building on St Croix, with its superb collection of Indian artefacts, and Wim Great House, which is a curious moated former estate building, excellently restored. Fort Christian on St Thomas houses an excellent museum, and St John is worthy of its national park.

Accommodation and dive operations VI Divers are associated with the Hotel Caravelle on St Croix, and Waves at Cane Bay also offer excellent diving close by. St Thomas Diving Club at the Bolongo Inclusive Beach Resort offers dive packages to reefs just 15 minutes from Bolongo Bay. Chris Sawyer Dive Centre on St Thomas offers trips to the *Rhone* in the British Virgin Islands, and Low Key Watersports operate in St John from Wharfside Village.

Emergency information Recompression chamber is at St Thomas Hospital in Charlotte Amalie, St Thomas Island, tel: (809) 776 8311; emergency tel: 922.

Formerly known as the Danish West Indies, the US Virgin Islands lie a few miles southeast of Tortola, although in reality they are worlds apart. Across The Narrows lies St John, one of three main islands in the 50-island group. Due east of St John, on the other side of Pillsbury Sound, is St Thomas and about 64km (40 miles) south lies the largest of the Virgin Islands, St Croix. Often called 'the American Paradise', the islands are a tropical 'home from home' for many Americans. After strolling down the main street of Charlotte Amalie, the capital of St Thomas, you feel as if you could be virtually anywhere in America.

Of the US Virgin Islands, St Thomas is the main one and the most developed. Much of the business is centred in Charlotte Amalie and its huge natural harbour. Government House, once the seat of the Danish Council, stands above the town centre. Virtually all of the surrounding hillsides are dotted with houses and the beaches are all developed with a huge variety of watersports on offer. Thatch Cay, to the north, is the largest of the smaller satellites, with Outer and Inner Brass, Saba Island, and Water, Birsk, Capella, and Great St James islands all popular for scuba diving.

St John is the smallest, and least developed, of the three main islands, and is also considered to be one of the most beautiful with its steep, lush, volcanic interior and fabulous beaches. Two-thirds of the island is given over to the Virgin Islands National Park, which has several trails leading through it as well as camping grounds, for those who do not wish to stay in one of the more sumptuous resorts. The largest of the offshore islets are Congo Cay, Leduck Island and Grass Cay.

St Croix (pronounced 'Saint Croy'), at 130km² (82 square miles) the largest of all the Virgin Islands, lies alone and entirely within the Caribbean. Formerly planted with sugar cane by the early Danish settlers, the land is now dotted with ruins and has been taken over by dairy and cattle-breeding farms. In the northeast, the capital of Christiansted is set on a bay filled with yachts, and protected by an offshore reef called Long Reef. The other main town, Frederiksted, is on the west coast and offers some delightful diving off the old pier. One of the best beaches is on Buck Island, a national park.

Although this book is primarily a diving guide, the Virgin Islands are in fact much better known for yachting. Due to the volcanic nature of these granitic islands, there is deep water close to shore and literally thousands of sheltered bays and inlets, allowing for some of the safest yachting conditions in the Caribbean.

With over 1.8 million visitors to the islands each year, you should expect a sophisticated economy, based on tourism, and a wide range of accommodation, resorts and facilities.

Opposite The nurse shark *(Ginglymostoma cirratum)* often rests during the day in the shelter of coral boulders.
Top The fingerprint cyphoma *(Cyphoma signatum)* is rare and mostly found in mating pairs on soft corals.

The Tunnels

Lying off Thatch Cay to the west of the Pillsbury Channel, The Tunnels are one of a series of caverns that cut into the island. Connected in several areas, they form interesting swim-throughs and caves. In the more shaded areas, you will see golden cup corals (*Tubastrea coccinea*) interspersed with brilliantly coloured sponges (remember to carry a torch to pick out the colours). Also

within the deeper recesses of the caves you will find glassy sweepers (*Pempheris schomburgki*), while the mouths of the caverns are festooned with sea fans, sea whips and hard corals. You can always find cleaning gobies (*Gobiosoma genie*) sitting on star coral (*Monastrea cavernosa*), waiting for various species of fish to line up and be cleaned of parasites and dead or decaying skin or scales.

The Yellow Brick Road

Between Congo Cay and Lovango Cay, north of Pillsbury Channel, is a sand chute known as The Yellow Brick Road. Diamond shapes in the sand indicate resting southern stingrays (*Dasyatis americana*), some of which may let you pet them, but remove your gloves first so as not to damage the protective mucus covering their skin. Peacock flounders (*Bothus lunatus*) as well as eyed flounders (*Bothus ocellatus*) can be seen here, and also burrowing sea urchins. Sand tile fish (*Malacanthus plumieri*) nest in the coral rubble and spotted eagle rays swim overhead.

Above Purple and yellow juvenile Spanish hogfish (*Bodianus rufus*) act as 'cleaners' to larger fish.

Top Fairy basslets (*Gramma loreto*) are brilliantly coloured fish, always found in shaded overhangs.

Map labels:
Congo Cay
Thatch Cay
The Tunnels
Yellow Brick Road
St Thomas
Pillsbury Channel
Witshoal Wreck
Charlotte Amalie
Saba Island
Water Island
Great St James Island
Little St James Island
US VIRGIN ISLANDS
Capella Island
Frenchcap Cay

Witshoal Wreck

The *West Indies Trader*, often referred to as the *Witshoal*, is located upright in 27m (90ft) of water, southwest of Charlotte Amalie. The 120m-long (400ft) boat is now a patchwork of golden cup corals, soft and hard corals, sea fans and whips, and sponges of every conceivable shape, colour and size. The maximum depth is 27m (90ft) to the sandy sea bed and only 11m (35ft) to the top of the wheelhouse. A twisted crane can be seen on the rear deck and the propellors are still intact. Moray eels are common, and an ever-present cloud of snapper and grunt, blue chromis and jacks, parrotfish and wrasse, which inhabit the various levels of the ship and its hanging cables.

Frenchcap Cay

From St Thomas it takes 40 minutes by boat to reach Frenchcap Cay south-west of Great St James Island, often in turbu-lent conditions created by currents that shift round the offshore islands to the south of Pillsbury Sound. The Pinnacles on the eastern side of the cay are home to several nurse sharks (*Ginglymo-stoma cirratum*), which can be seen resting under the coral ledges during the day. If you are lucky enough to dive this site at night, you may encounter them on the reef, hunting lobster and

octopus. The Pinnacles are a series of towering boulders, home to all kinds of corals and sponges. The Cathedrals, on the western side of the cay, are great for a second dive; a vertical cut into the rock opens into a large natural chamber, illuminated by a shaft of light which reaches the sea floor. The walls are ablaze with cup corals and sponges, so remember your torch.

Top The coney (*Cephalopholis fulva*) has three colour phases; note these bicolour markings.

Above Fairy basslets have similar colouring to hogfish, with a deep indigo head and yellow tail.

Cane Bay

On the north shore of St Croix, about a 25-minute drive west from Christiansted, popular Cane Bay has a superb coral wall which starts about 100m (328ft) from the shore. In the shallows, at around 15m (50ft), are the Cane Bay Gardens, a very well-developed coral field of many different varieties, including Venus sea fans (*Gorgonia flabellum*) and wide-mesh sea fans (*Gorgonia mariae*). Look closely at the fans, because you should be able to find one of the most common

molluscs in the Caribbean, the flamingo tongue (*Cyphoma gibbosum*), feeding on the coral polyps. This coral garden eventually evolves into the classic hills and valleys of a spur-and-groove reef, which crowns at 15m (50ft) before dropping gradually into the depths.

Steeply sloping Cane Bay Wall has many hard and soft corals, as well as some very long lavender tube sponges (*Callyspongia vaginalis*). Among the coral overhangs are brilliantly coloured fairy basslet (*Gramma loreto*), as well as squirrelfish, bigeye and butterflyfish. Peppermint gobies (*Coryphopterus lipernes*) perch on brain corals and juvenile hogfish and blue-headed wrasse set up cleaning stations for passing customers.

Above Caribbean reef squid (*Sepioteuthis sepioidea*) can usually be spotted on all night dives around the shallow fringing reefs of the Virgin Islands.

Left The giant featherduster worm (*Sabellastarte magnifica*) is the largest Caribbean tube worm.

Opposite Azure vase sponges (*Callyspongia plicifera*) are commonly found on shallow reefs.

THE GULF ISLANDS

Geographically at the northern limit of the Caribbean Sea, north of the Greater Antilles and the Leeward Islands, is the vast expanse of water known as the Gulf of Mexico. However, the Caribbean is largely regarded as all of the area between North and South America, and for this reason we have included Turks and Caicos, the Bahamas and Bermuda. The reasons for their inclusion are that the waters which feed all these islands with rich nutrients and plankton have a common source known as the Gulf Stream. It flows through the northern Caribbean, past the Turks and Caicos, the Bahamas and the Florida Keys, then sweeps up to the northern Atlantic, creating the most northerly coral reef to be found in the world, Bermuda.

TURKS AND CAICOS

Saltpans, Dolphins and Humpback Whales

THE GULLEY • MUSHROOM WALL • THE AMPHITHEATRE • EEL GARDENS • MCDONALDS • LIBRARY

Located 925km (575 miles) south of Miami – a 90-minute flight away – are the Turks and Caicos, a group of 30 islands, only eight of which are inhabited. Set on two huge submarine peaks thrusting up from the ocean, the islands are separated by a 48km (30-mile) deep-water channel called Turks Islands Passage, which runs between Grand Turk and Salt Cay to the west and the Caicos group to the east.

Now a British crown colony, the islands were first settled by Lucayan and Arawak Indians, and then later discovered by Columbus. The Caicos Islands (the word is derived from the Spanish *caya*, meaning 'small island') were largely unpopulated till 1670, when Spain ceded them to Britain. Bermudan saltrakers established the first colonies on Grand Turk and Salt Cay, and salt was the primary industry for 300 years. It was exchanged for other goods in trading with Bermuda and the east coast of America, thus creating the original 'Bermuda Triangle' – that of commerce.

Less than 10km (6 miles) long and barely a kilometre wide, Grand Turk is a remnant of sleepy old-style colonialism with several hotels on the west coast having been converted from charming 19th-century homes. The vertical wall northwest of the island is just a 10-minute boat ride away. In many spots you can actually swim out from the shore, but it is preferable to use a local dive boat.

Diving on Salt Cay (a UNESCO World Heritage Site), is concentrated at the southern and northern ends of the island. The shipwreck *Endymion*, further to the south beyond Sand Cay, is proving to be a drawcard for more exploratory divers.

HMS *Endymion* was a twin-deck man o' war, built in Limehouse on the Thames in 1779. The 42m-long (140ft) schooner struck a reef and sank on Saturday, 28 August 1790. Luckily the reef was shallow and none of the crew was lost. They stayed with the ship for three days before setting off in three small support craft to Grand Turk. The ship's remains are scattered among three sections of a spur-and-groove reef, her anchors and 44 guns clearly visible.

Providenciales (or Provo), one of the Caicos islands, is twice the size of Bermuda and the most developed island in the chain. Though the British influence is noticeable, it is reminiscent of Florida, with multimillion-dollar developments all over – raising land values but lowering the island's appeal in many ways. The northwest wall, 40 minutes by boat from the shore, is where most diving takes place. Similar in distance, but offering far better diving, is the western wall of West Caicos – a favourite with underwater photographers. In many locations, the wall drops vertically from 12m (40ft) and often has huge underhanging gardens of coral and colourful sponges.

Best time to go The hottest months are Sep–Oct, with temperatures soaring to 35°C (95°F); this is also hurricane season. Apr–May is generally quiet with more space on the dive boats; avoid holiday weekends.

Getting there There are direct flights twice daily on American Airlines from Miami to Providenciales, and from Miami to Grand Turk at weekends.

Special interest The Maritime Museum is superb, with excellent exhibits on ancient Amerindian culture and the history of the Turks and Caicos. Providenciales has the only commercial conch farm in the Caribbean. Regarded as a national treasure, JoJo the dolphin can be seen most days near the Club Med and Ocean Club resort. Little Water Cay, only accessible by boat, has a huge population of quite friendly iguanas.

Accommodation and dive operations At Turtle Cove on Provo, there are three operations: Turtle In Divers, Flamingo Divers and Art Pickering's Turtle Divers. Turtle Divers are located within the Turtle Cove Inn, which has one of the best restaurants in the Caribbean. Seaeye Diving and Oasis Divers are on Grand Turk and guests can stay at the Salt Raker Inn, Grand Turk Inn or Guanahani Beach Resort.

Electricity supply American-style plugs, 120V, for recharging dive lights and flashes.

Emergency information Recompression chamber at the Ewan Menzies Medical Centre on Provo, tel: 64242 or 64321.

Previous pages Treasure Cay in the Bahamas is a superb destination for both divers and sun worshippers.
Opposite The coral drop-off on West Caicos is renowned for having some of the best diving in the Caribbean.
Top Orange ball anemones (*Pseudocorynactis caribbeorum*) are a favourite of photographers on Grand Turk.

The Gulley, West Caicos

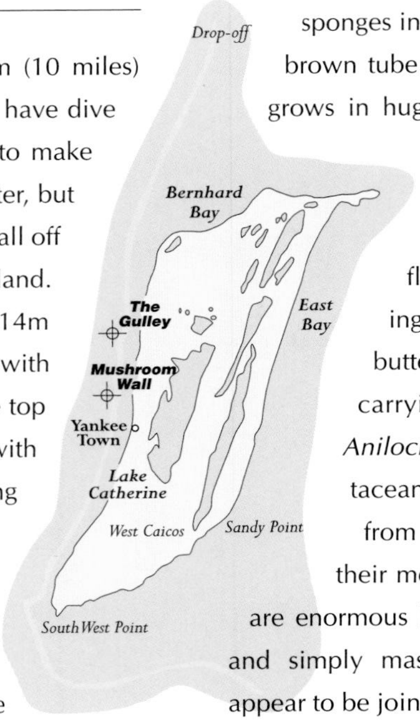

The island of West Caicos lies 16km (10 miles) southwest of Provo. Most dive shops have dive boats located to the south of Provo to make the journey time to West Caicos shorter, but it still takes 40 minutes to reach the wall off the western, rugged coast of the island. The lip of the reef folds over at 14m (47ft) and drops into a narrow gulley with overhanging corals and sponges. The top of the reef is particularly healthy, with some very large shoals, containing several hundred individuals, of snapper and grunt. In the gulley, which is actually a narrow sand chute, there are some huge stands of black coral (*Antipathes* sp.). Wire coral (*Cirrhipathes leutkeni*) spirals upwards towards the light and there is an entangled jumble of different coloured rope sponges (*Aplysina cauliformis* and *Aplysina fulva*).

[Map labels: Drop-off; Bernhard Bay; East Bay; The Gulley; Mushroom Wall; Yankee Town; Lake Catherine; West Caicos; Sandy Point; South West Point]

Mushroom Wall, West Caicos

Named after the curious water-carved, mushroom-shaped ancient coralline ironstone reef on the shoreline, Mushroom Wall is similar in profile to the Gulley, but the outer edge of the reef is much more convoluted and with more massive sponges in shallower water, particularly the brown tube sponge (*Agelas conifera*) which grows in huge clumps, some several metres high. Snapper and grunt are common on the reef top and there are also plenty of butterflyfish and angelfish. It is interesting to note the numbers of foureye butterflyfish (*Chaetodon capistratus*) carrying groupings of the parasite *Anilocra laticaudata* (a type of crustacean that lives on the blood it sucks from its host), attached to the sides of their mouths, eyes and gill plates. There are enormous black corals, gorgonian sea fans and simply massive barrel sponges. All these appear to be joined together by rope sponges, and dotted with fairy basslets (*Gramma loreto*).

The Amphitheatre, Northwest Wall

This is a spectacular dive on the northwest wall of Provo, about 40 minutes by boat from Turtle Cove. Before reaching the drop-off, you may meet a school of Atlantic spadefish (*Chaetodipterus faber*) which sweeps in gracefully amid the coral and sponge uprights. The top of the reef rolls over at 12m (40ft) and folds into a natural amphitheatre at 21m (69ft) with a sandy bottom and a raised lip of sheet corals on the outward edge. Naturally curved around the wall, this is a splendid site to spend some time and watch large barracuda and black jacks (*Caranx lugubris*) as they hunt singly or in small packs of three or four individuals.

On either side of the Amphitheatre, the reef curves down to smaller sand shelves at 31m (103ft), where nurse sharks rest in the morning. The reef is deeply undercut by hanging corals and sponges, with some huge specimens of the orange elephant's ear sponge (*Agelas clathrodes*). In fact, the Turks and Caicos are known to have the largest specimens of this sponge in the Caribbean.

As you ascend to the lip of the near vertical wall, you will see shoals of snapper and grunt. In the shallows in front of the mooring buoy, there are sand tile fish, small sand blennies, and virtually all of the coral heads are home to cleaning stations with gobies perched on the star and brain corals, waiting for clients.

Below left The cryptic teardrop crab (*Pelia mutica*) likes to attach small sponges, algae and tunicates to its shell as camouflage.

Below The black-spotted sea goddess (*Hypselodoris bayeri*) is a colourful nudibranch of the Gulf Islands.

Eel Gardens
Northwest Wall, Providenciales

Further south from the Amphitheatre, the reef drops less steeply, but still plummets away beyond the safe diving limit. The wall curves around to the south and is covered in a forest of gorgonian sea fans and plumes. Hard corals are much more evident here, particularly sheet corals (*Agaricia grahamae* and *Agaricia lamarki*). Stove-pipe sponges (*Aplysina archeri*) are everywhere and small hermit crabs can be seen crawling over them. Gorgonian sea fans seem to come in many different forms, stretched out perpendicular to the wall. On the inner sandy area around 10m (33ft) a large colony of garden eels (*Heteroconger halis*) can be found; this gives the site its name. They are shy fish, retreating into their holes as you approach them. If you keep back, they rise so far out of their holes that they sway in the current, picking off plankton with a jerking movement of their heads.

Top and above At night, sea rods and plumes are home to tufted nudibranchs *(Tritoniopsis frydis)* and white-speckled nudibranchs *(Phyllodesmium spp.)*.

Below Lettuce sea slugs *(Tridachia crispata)* are algae feeders and are quite common in the Caribbean.

Above Fireworms *(Hermodice carunculata),* seen here draped over sea plumes, should be avoided because of the barbed hairs along the sides of their bodies.

Below Star horseshoe worms *(Pomatostegus stellatus)* can be found on all the hard corals.

McDonalds, Grand Turk

This very popular site has an abundant growth of healthy corals and sponges, with the shallowest part of the reef being approximately 9m (30ft), making it ideal for beginners. A natural archway of overlapping corals atop a sand chute has created a rather interesting feature at 18m (60ft). Although fish feeding is now frowned upon, the fish in this area have always been fed in the past and continue to be friendly to divers, but now without their more aggressive tendencies. Because of the light, the site is best dived around midday or early in the afternoon and is therefore perfect as a second dive. The outer coral ridge drops vertically from around 12m (40ft) and has a huge array of sponges and gorgonians.

Below Spotted moray eels (*Gymnothorax moringa*) are common in the Turks and Caicos Islands.

Library, Grand Turk

Located on the edge of the reef wall directly opposite where the old Grand Turk library used to be in Cockburn Town, the Library is one of Grand Turk's most popular dives. The back of the reef is rather flat and rocky with relatively little coral and sponge growth. Coral-encrusted ballast stones form small rocky reefs, a remnant of old saltraker days, until you reach the lip of the wall, which starts at 6m (20ft). Although this site is mostly used for beginners and is considered to be somewhat bland during the day, at night it is a mecca for invertebrate marine life.

Using powerful dive lights, this vertical drop literally lights up with golden cup corals (*Tubastrea coccinea*), which only open their feeding polyps at night. There are also orange ball anemones – considered quite a rare find in many other areas of the Caribbean – and thousands of Christmas-tree and featherduster worms. Arrow crabs (*Stenorhynchus seticornis*) sit on sponges and corals, waving their violet-tipped pincers at the plankton attracted by the lights. Pufferfish can be seen, as well as octopus, spotted lobsters, banded coral shrimps (*Stenopus hispidus*) and, in all the recesses, the green, gleaming eyes of the red night shrimp (*Rhynchocinetes rigens*).

Moray eels are common, mainly the spotted (*Gymnothorax moringa*) and the goldentail (*Gymnothorax miliaris*) morays. Amid the sea fans there are harlequin pipefish (*Micrognathus crinitus*) and tiny cryptic teardrop crabs (*Pelia mutica*). Perched on the tube sponges and sea fans, each of these tiny spider crabs is adorned with minute sponges and hydroids.

Above Goldentail moray eels *(Gymnothorax miliaris)* are very timid and only rarely seen at night.

Below The largest of the morays is the green moray eel *(Gymnothorax funebris)*, an active feeder at night.

THE QUEEN CONCH

Now a protected species in Bermuda and Florida, the queen conch *(Strombus gigas)* is the staple food of many eastern Caribbean islanders. It is popular among tourists, who not only want to eat the flesh of this supposed aphrodisiac, but want the shell as a souvenir.

Conch shells (pronounced 'konk') are very common around the shallow sand flats of the Bahama Banks. The only commercial conch farm exists in Turks and Caicos – this farm not only supplies the growing food trade, but is also instrumental in seeding areas of shallow sand flats in other countries where the conch has been virtually wiped out by blatant commercialism and a disregard for any conservation policies.

Conchs are social marine molluscs and have some of the largest shells found in the Caribbean. Specimens of different sizes and ages live in close proximity to each other, and they often overlap during mating. When they are about four years old, they reach sexual maturity and, during the period from March to November, can lay several egg clusters consisting of a quarter of a million eggs. In the Turks and Caicos farm, the same pair of conchs has been supplying the egg ribbons over a period of years.

The young, or veliger, are free swimming. They hatch after after a few weeks, and join the millions of other planktonic creatures moving through the Caribbean in the Gulf Stream. This greatly spreads the distribution, and when the young find a suitable habitat, they quickly settle and start the cycle once more. As the shell develops, it loses its external decoration and produces a strong, thick lip, the underside of which is a beautiful pink. In the Bahamas it is forbidden to collect conchs without this developed lip.

The adult conch has very few predators other than man. For centuries its shell has been used as decoration by Taino, Arawak and Lucayan Indians, the original settlers of the Caribbean. Now all the market stalls throughout the Caribbean sell conch shells as a by-product of the commercial food industry.

The flesh of the conch is removed from its shell by hammering a hole into its base. This cuts the muscular foot, thus releasing the animal. The foot is then tenderized by hammering it and placing it in a marinade. The flesh is low in fat and carbohydrates. They are preferable, however, lumbering about the shallow sand flats of Caribbean reefs.

Above The queen conch *(Strombus gigas)* is one of the largest gastropods in the world.

THE BAHAMAS

Shark Encounters, Dolphins and Fabulous Walls

UNEXSO • JAMES BOND WRECKS • THEO'S WRECK • SHARK ALLEY • CONCEPTION ISLAND

Discovered in 1492 by Columbus, the Bahamas straddle the Tropic of Cancer and consist of 700 islands and 2500 small cays, scattered across over 160,000km² (100,000 square miles) of ocean.

Originally called Bajamar (meaning 'shallow seas') by Columbus, the name eventually evolved to Bahama. Geologically, the Bahamas are the tips of a huge plateau that was more than 90m (300ft) above sea level during the last ice age. As the ice melted, the waters rose, transforming the plateau into a vast series of shallow, submerged banks. The larger islands are New Providence, Andros and Grand Bahama. They are all home to some of the most varied and spectacular diving in the Caribbean, and offer excellent visibility, warm waters, wrecks, caverns, blue holes, an abundance of fish, stingrays, dolphins and, of course, shark encounters.

Shark diving in the Bahamas started 20 years ago off Long Island. It is often referred to as 'pay and display' diving, or as a spectator sport. Divers are positioned in a semicircle and sit in stunned (if rather scary) silence as large groups of Caribbean reef sharks come in and take bait from the experienced shark wranglers dressed in chain-mail suits.

On Walkers Cay, at Undersea Adventures in the Abacos, they have developed a similar ritualized feed, during which hundreds of sharks attack a large frozen bait ball called a 'chumsickle' that is lowered into the middle of a group of nervous and awe-struck divers. Hammerhead sharks vie for scraps and space with Caribbean reef sharks, shortfin mako, lemon, bull, nurse, and tiger sharks. Though it is not for the faint-hearted, this is one of the best shark dives in the Bahamas.

Possibly the greatest variety of shark encounters takes place south of Nassau, the Bahamas capital based on New Providence Island – from the controlled feeds offered by Stuart Cove's Dive South Ocean to the excitement of entering the water as part of a two-tank dive trip to the Shark Wall and Runway. The US Navy Buoy is another site used by Stuart Cove, where you can dive with silky sharks, which are attracted to life around the buoy.

Nearby Andros is another favoured location for exploratory diving; here, huge blue holes have been discovered, linking the open sea to holes in the island. Rob Palmer's Blue Holes Foundation is at the leading edge of this exploration and, while some of the diving is particularly challenging, the rewards are fantastic.

In the southern island chains, San Salvador (see page 144) lays claim to being the original landfall of Columbus and has some truly spectacular wall diving. The Exumas and Acklin Islands form an unspoilt paradise and at least six live-aboard boats work here, some concentrating on wall diving and others on shark and dolphin encounters.

Best time to go Nov–Jun are the driest months; Jul–Oct is hurricane season and has the most rainfall. Jul–Aug can be very busy, so book well in advance, especially for the shark dives and Dolphin Experience.

Getting there Regular international flights leave weekly from the UK and Europe on all the major air carriers. There are numerous daily flights from most of the major USA airports. These fly into Nassau or Freeport with inter-island connections to the rest of the Bahama chain on Bahamasair.

Special interest The Dolphin Experience at UNEXSO has to be on everyone's list, offering the opportunity to dive in the open ocean with dolphins.

Accommodation and dive operations Stuart Cove's Dive South Ocean is next to the South Ocean Club, and Nassau Scuba Centre is associated with the Orange Hill Club. UNEXSO has arrangements with all of the Freeport hotels. Walkers Cay has its own hotel and marina, as does Stella Maris on Long Island and the Riding Rock Inn on San Salvador. For specialist blue hole expeditions, contact Rob Palmer's Blue Holes Foundation, which also uses the Small Hope Bay Lodge on Andros.

Electricity supply American-style plugs, 110V at 60 cycles.

Emergency information The Bahamas' main recompression chamber is located at UNEXSO in Freeport, Grand Bahama Island, tel: (242) 373 1244.

Opposite The stern and propeller of Theo's wreck are encrusted with golden cup corals and small sponges.
Top The shallow coral is covered in beautiful sea fans, which look delicate but are extremely robust.

UNEXSO

UNEXSO (The Underwater Exploration Society) at Freeport on Grand Bahama Island is the oldest, most established diving centre in the Bahamas. With 30 years' experience, it offers a diversity of diving. There is a daily shark-feeding programme out at Shark Junction, just 10 minutes by boat from the dock. A detailed lecture is given before each trip and divers are made aware of the risks involved with hand-feeding large wild animals.

On first entering the water, you are positioned in front of an old recompression chamber and as the shark feeder arrives with a container full of fish, he is soon surrounded by snapper, grouper, horse-eyed jacks, amberjacks, stingrays, nurse sharks and Caribbean reef sharks (*Carcharhinus perezi*). Safety divers position themselves at the edges of the group and the shark feeder, dressed in a chain-mail suit, controls the action – the bait is kept in an enclosed PVC tube.

The sharks rush in and out of the feeding area, taking the bait from the shark feeder's hand and in some cases, he will stroke the sharks – particularly the larger females. These sharks not only react to feeding, they also love the tactile sensation. The sharks come to well within arm's reach of the spectators, and divers are requested to resist the temptation to touch them.

Right and below Abundant numbers of Caribbean reef sharks *(Carcharhinus perezi)* are attracted to the UNEXSO shark feed which takes place daily off Grand Bahama. Divers are requested to keep absolutely still as the sharks rush into the feeding arena to take the bait. The sharks are then handfed by experienced shark wranglers wearing protective chain-mail suits.

Besides the shark dives, UNEXSO also takes divers to reefs, walls and wrecks. It is famous, too, for its involvement in a programme called Dolphin Experience where tourists on the surface, as well as divers underwater, are given the opportunity to interact with bottlenose dolphins (*Tursiops truncatus*).

The dolphins are essentially habitualized and some young have been born in captivity. They are allowed out into the open ocean each day, although they are usually held in pens for their own safety and for the entertainment of tourists. The dolphins quite often want nothing to do with people and will take off on their own to feed around the reefs and interact with a local pod of wild dolphins.

Opposite By far the most captivating of all animal encounters are those between dolphins in the wild; these are spotted dolphins (*Stenella plagiodon*).

Above and right At the Dolphin Experience on Grand Bahama, divers are given the exhilarating opportunity to play with bottlenose dolphins (*Tursiops truncatus*) in the open ocean.

To beat the boats with their camera-waving cargo of so-called ecotourists and offspring, we had to leave the dock at 5:30. We were hoping to photograph the manatees in their wintering ground in Crystal River, Florida. But if we arrived after 7:00, we risked sharing their company with 50 or 60 other visitors, disgorged by the boats and intent on playing with these gentle giants.

Manatees fascinate tourists as they have fascinated man for centuries. Hundreds of years ago, mariners believed that manatees and their cousins, the dugongs, were the mermaids perpetuated in legends today. Indeed, the word for their family group, Sirenians, recalls the name 'sirens' – mythical mermaids believed by the ancient Greeks to have lured ships and sailors to their destruction. Today, though, it is these living 'mermaids' that are in danger of dying.

Manatees have been on the official endangered species list since 1973 and they are a particularly difficult creature to protect. One of the reasons for this is their gentleness when approached, another is their utmost disregard for danger. But perhaps the key cause for their plight is their lifestyle.

The manatee, or sea cow (*Trichechus manatus latirostris*), is found on coastal and inland waterways from Brazil in South America to Virginia in the United States. Known in Guatemala, Belize, the southern coast of the Yucatán in Mexico and Hispaniola, they can be found around a number of Caribbean islands. Recent very rare sightings include off Harbour Island in the northern Bahamas and off Grand Turk. Their most common location, however, is on the northwest coast of Florida.

Manatees are the largest vegetarians in the sea; they weigh over 1361kg (3000 lb) and grow to a length of 4m (13ft). They are often mistakenly taken to be a cross between a seal and a whale, but are in fact relatives of the elephant: you can clearly see the 'fingernails' at the end of each flipper.

Above The manatee *(Trichechus manatus latirostris)* is incredibly friendly, with no natural enemies other than man.

Right Manatees form large social groups during the winter months and congregate in the vicinity of Crystal River, where a constant warm water source can be found.

Fossil evidence indicates that ancient relatives of the present-day species have been around for millennia and that there were once more than a dozen species of sea cow. Stellar's sea cow, the largest of all the sea cows, from the Bering Sea was exterminated in 1786 by Russian explorers and hunters. There are now only four species left: the Amazon, West African and West Indian manatees, and the dugong. All of the species have been hunted virtually to extinction for their meat, oil, skin, teeth and even their tears. They are now being additionally threatened by encroachment on their environment, and even more alarming is a new virus which is having a devastating effect on the adult population along the southwest Florida coast.

As the temperature of the shallow water along Florida's west coast drops in winter, the manatees slowly make their way through the coastal waters to the warm springs inland, following the source of the constant 72°F (22°C) water, where they will spend their winter months. This annual migration is necessary for their survival – when the temperature of the coastal reed beds drops, so does their food source.

FLORIDA KEYS

Cutting a swathe across the direction of the Gulf Stream, the Florida Keys are located to the south of the gigantic sand bar which is Florida, the principal tourism state for the USA. Juan Ponce de Leon originally discovered the mainland in 1512 at Easter (known in Spain as *Flores*), so he decided to call the land La Florida. Even in those early days, the reefs and shoals of the Florida Keys played havoc with the Spanish fleet, and today treasure salvors such as Mel Fisher have reaped the benefits by discovering reefs of silver bullion, gold coins and emeralds.

Now the 200 or so Keys have a treasure of marine life as well as some claims to fame. Key West, where Ernest Hemingway spent so much of his life, is the starting point of the first principal highway in the United States, US1 Highway, which stretches for 180km (115 miles) and crosses 42 bridges. Key Largo, to the north of the chain, is where America's first marine national park was founded in 1960. Although it is a very strict conservation area, it is open to all divers and snorkellers, who have to travel by boat to reefs located several kilometres offshore.

To commemorate America's first official marine reserve, the Pennekamp National Marine Park, a bronze statue called *The Christ of the Abyss* was settled underwater at a site called Dry Rock. Stationed on a concrete block in 7.5m (24ft) of water, the Christ statue's head is thrown back, facing the surface, his arms outstretched. Now an incredibly popular site for snorkellers and divers, the statue is a focal point amidst a sheltered area of reef which has resident large green moray eels and schools of snapper and grunt. The nearby coral canyons are home to numerous spiny lobsters, arrow crabs and anemones.

Right The *Christ of the Abyss* was placed underwater to commemorate the Pennekamp National Marine Park, the first such reserve in the United States.

Named after Theodopolis Galanoupoulos, an engineer who worked for shipowners, the Bahama Cement Company, Theo's Wreck was built in Norway in 1954 and was originally called the MS *Logna*, and then the MV *Island Cement*. When the time came for scrapping the ship, Theo suggested deliberately sinking the ship as an artificial reef. With the help of UNEXSO, she was sunk on 16 October 1982, off the Silver Beach Inlet

James Bond Wrecks

The south shore of New Providence Island has been featured in a number of Hollywood block-buster movies, including several James Bond films. Nearby Stuart Cove's Dive South Ocean (which was rebuilt for the set of the film, *Flipper*), there are several wrecks sunk deliberately by Stuart Cove as props for James Bond. *Never Say Never Again* called for a wreck named the *Tears Of Allah*, a 30m (100ft) former drug-runner seized by the Bahamian Government. She now sits upright in 15m (50ft) of water and is gradually being covered in marine growth.

The most spectacular site here is the scaffolding that held the structure of the Vulcan bomber which featured in *Thunderball*. Now resembling an underwater 'jungle gym', the scaffolding is covered in virtually every species of gorgonian sea fan and soft coral to be found in the Caribbean; this is invertebrate heaven and photographers

return to this location time after time to film arrow crabs, lima file clams, filefish, cleaner shrimps, nudibranchs, and snails. Small grouper, snapper, grunt, trumpetfish and parrotfish abound above this incredible artificial reef.

Nearby are a number of other wrecks, including the *WiLLaurie*. Built in 1908 and sunk by Stuart Cove in 1988, this is one of the best night dives in the Bahamas, offering octopus, large grouper, nudi-branchs, shrimps, snails, and golden cup corals. The top of the hold's skeleton superstructure is overhung with sea plumes, sponges and fans.

Above The *Papa Doc* wreck off Grand Bahama is now home to thousands of silverside minnows.

Right The remaining scaffolding of the film prop used in the film *Thunderball* is now a veritable mass of soft corals and sponges.

off Grand Bahama Island. Now resting on her port side, she lies in 29–33m (95–110ft) of water with her stern clear of the sea bed and facing a drop-off, the Grand Bahama Ledge. Looking up through the propellor and rudder, the shaded underside is a carpet of golden cup corals (*Tubastrea coccinea*). There are safe entry points in the bridge and accommodation section and the hold is completely open, allowing free access for sport divers. In front of the accommodation section a large and friendly resident green moray

eel (*Gymnothorax funebris*) often frightens divers, and several species of angelfish, swimming in their lifelong mating pairs, can be seen here.

The superstructure of the ship is now covered in both soft and hard corals, as well as deep water sea fans which stretch out into the current, and large schools of snapper and grunt congregate around the bows and the still recognizable winches on the foredeck. Divers must be very careful not to hold onto the rails, as they are covered in marine life including stinging hydroids,

small tunicates and sponges. Although this is a deep dive with limited bottom time, Theo's Wreck is highly commended, particularly at night when large numbers of huge rainbow parrotfish (*Scarus guacamaia*) can be found there, sleeping peacefully on the superstructure.

Below Theo's Wreck, lying south of Grand Bahama Island, has been earmarked as a future marine reserve by the Bahamas National Trust.

SAN SALVADOR

Located 320km (200 miles) east-southeast of Nassau and southeast of Cat Island, San Salvador was where Christopher Columbus made his original landfall on 12 October 1492. Known as Guanahani by the local Arawak Indians ('Men from Heaven', as the locals called the Spanish!), Columbus knelt on the white powder sand beach and claimed the land for Spain. Now, San Salvador also stands head and shoulders (in diving terms) above the other 'Family Islands' of the outer Bahamas chain. Although the island is quite small at 20km (12 miles) long by 8 km (5 miles) wide and is circumnavigated by the Queen's Highway, San Salvador is known today as the top wall diving destination in the Bahamas. It is famous for its crystal-clear, flat, calm waters, and divers are now discovering its attractions. The walls are for the most part pristine and vertical in many areas, and all the dive sites have mooring buoys to prevent anchor damage.

The diving operators on the island have placed 48 mooring buoys above the island's dive sites and a further large number of sheltered sand holes, clear of any reefs, are used as anchor drops, primarily for snorkelling amidst the shallower patch reefs which are well protected from the worst of the weather. However, it is the outer vertical wall dives which are of the greatest interest, with sites such as the Telephone Pole, Devil's Claw and Double Caves offering absolutely outstanding scenic diving.

Above left San Salvador has what is probably the best diving on all of the Bahamas, with spectacular walls, caverns and gullies cutting the reef crest.

pelagic shark is encountered in the offshore waters of The Tongue of the Ocean, an 1800m-deep (6000ft) trench that bisects the Bahamas between New Providence Island and Andros Island. This is sold more as a 'natural' encounter between man and shark adrift in the ocean. Attracted by the buoy, many other species of fish also take refuge, which in turn attracts other predators; at the top of this food chain are the sharks, who in turn eventually arrive.

Conception Island

Located in the centre of the triangle created by Long Island to the west (where the Stella Maris Dive Resort is situated), Cat Island to the north and Rum Cay to the south, Conception Island keeps coming up as one of the top dive locations in the southern Bahamas chain. Uninhabited Conception Island has been declared a terrestrial and marine wildlife sanctuary by the Bahamas National Trust, due to the exceptional quality of the vertical walls which plummet into the depths around the island, and also for the large number of turtles which breed there.

Although considered by many to be too far out of the way, divers are now able to visit this remote island from Stella Maris, which takes between two and four hours, depending on the boat and the prevailing weather conditions; this makes it an all-day expedition. Although the wall dives are quite deep, the reef edge is riddled with caverns and tunnels, patrolled by barracuda, jacks and tuna, wherever the silversides shoal in summer. Every sea fan appears to hold flamingo tongue snails (*Cyphoma gibbosum*), surely the most common sea snail in the entire Caribbean. There are tiny filefish hiding in nooks and crannies amid the sea plumes and juvenile spotted drum (*Equetus*

Shark Alley

Stuart Cove has developed three distinct types of shark dive. At Shark Wall, divers enter the water on the lip of the oceanic trench which then drops to 1800m (6000ft). Here there are at least a dozen resident Caribbean reef sharks and several large grouper to accompany you on your dive along this coral wall, which is curiously lacking in other fish. On the second dive, the shark feeder leads you a short way in from the lip of the wall into a wide, sandy natural amphitheatre called the Shark Alley. Here, dressed in a full chain-mail suit, or at least chain-mail sleeves and gauntlets, the shark feeder uses a polespear to feed the sharks.

Once the sharks have taken the bait, they swim out of the feeding arena and then come down through an alleyway in the reef, so by gauging where the sharks are when they are feeding, you can enjoy face-to-face encounters with the sharks as they swim within touching distance via the alleyway back into the arena. (After the shark feed, look for dislodged shark teeth in the sand of the arena – a great souvenir.)

The Nassau dive operators also have a much freer encounter with sharks, particularly silky sharks (*Carcharhinus falciformis*). This smaller

Above Nassau groupers (*Epinephelus striatus*) are particularly friendly and photogenic.

punctatus) dancing under the coral overhangs. Orangesided gobies (*Gobiosoma dilephsis*) perch on top of sponges and razorfish dart into the sand just before the reef drops over the wall.

Some 11km (7 miles) north of Conception is Southampton Reef, an absolutely superb site with a forest of staghorn and elkhorn coral gardens, and an 80-year-old unnamed freighter covering around 300m² (1000 square feet).

Above Diamond blennies *(Malacoctenus boehlkei)* are timid fish, often seen around giant anemones.

Right Redlip blennies *(Ophioblennius atlanticus)* look rather comical when they perch on the tips of coral.

Below Creole-fish *(Paranthias furcifer)* are also timid fish, always hiding amidst tube sponges.

145

BERMUDA

The Northernmost Coral Reef in the World

CONSTELLATION AND NOLA WRECKS • EASTERN BLUE CUT • FLATTS BRIDGE

At the north of the notorious triangle of the same name, Bermuda is only 1040km (650 miles) east of Cape Hatteras in the USA and 6000km (3750 miles) from mainland Europe – or a seven-hour flight on British Airways from Gatwick in London. At one time, Bermuda would have been a single, fairly substantial island, before the level of the sea rose with the melting of the polar caps. Created with the formation of a gigantic volcano rising some 4500m (15,000ft) from the sea bed, the islands are the lower southeastern end of a former giant atoll. Some speculate that these islands could once have been the fabled Atlantis lying beyond the Pillars of Hercules.

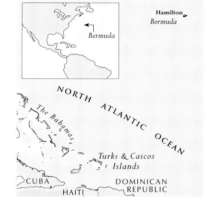

The Bermudas, or Bermudez, were originally claimed for Spain by Juan de Bermudez around 1511, but it is not known whether he set foot on *caya de demonios* – the 'Isles of Devils'. In 1492, when Columbus sailed the ocean, the trade winds would probably have carried him fairly close to the treacherous shores of Bermuda – it is just luck that he did not end up alongside the other 400 ships which have sunk amid the reefs and shoals surrounding these islands. In 1609 Admiral Sir George Somers was on his way to Jamestown, Virginia, when his fleet of nine ships was scattered during a hurricane. Somers' ship, the *Sea Venture*, was demasted and limped along in the direction of Bermuda, before gradually sinking. Somers and his crew salvaged what they could of the *Sea Venture* and, together with local wood, built the *Deliverance* and the *Patience,* in which they sailed on to Jamestown where they found pestilence, disease and famine compared to the 'earthly paradise' that they had just left behind. Word soon got back to Britain and the first colonists arrived on the islands in 1612.

Fed by the warm waters of the Gulf Stream, Bermuda's coral reefs are the most northerly in the world, with much of the same marine life as in the eastern Caribbean. Bermuda is now regarded as the Caribbean's top wreck diving location. It is the only place in the world where you can dive on shipwrecks spanning five centuries, all easily accessible in shallow water.

The main bodies of water surrounding the islands include the Great and Little Sounds which lead into Hamilton Harbour; St Georges Harbour, on the other side of the airport; and Castle Harbour at the Causeway, where a number of islets stop the ocean swell from breaking over the sand flats. One of these is Nonsuch Island, where William Bebe carried out some of the earliest deep water experiments in a diving bell. Last but not least is Harrington Sound, a massive inland sea fed only through a narrow gap at Flatts Bridge where the tidal race can reach up to 3.5 knots; at slack water, the shore diving under the bridge is probably the best in the Bermudas.

Best time to go Apr–Jun and Oct–Nov are the best times. Humidity is high in mid-summer and water temperatures range from 17–26°C (63–79°F).

Getting there Four flights per week with British Airways from Gatwick in London. Condor have a weekly (Tue) direct flight from Frankfurt as well as connections on American airlines from JFK and Florida.

Special interest Save the last of your dollars and go to the Swizzle Inn for Rum Swizzles – a lethal combination of rum and fruit juice. The Bermuda Dockyards and the Maritime Museum are excellent, with a fine display of the island's past. Flatt's Bridge Aquarium and Zoo, at the entrance to Harrington Sound, has a display on the most northerly coral reef in the world.

Accommodation and dive operations Blue Water Divers at Robinson's Marina, Somerset Bridge, is the closest dive shop to Lantana and Cambridge Beaches. Fantasea Divers are located near Greenbank Cottages, and South Side Scuba along the south shore at the Sonesta Hotel and close to Longtail Cliffs Apartments. Nautilus Diving Ltd is located at the Southampton Princess Hotel, and Scuba Look is attached to the Grotto Bay Hotel near the causeway to the airport.

Emergency information The recompression chamber is located at King Edwards Memorial Hospital, Point Finger Road and Berry Road, Paget, Bermuda. Emergency tel: (441) 236 2345.

Opposite Bermuda has excellent wreck diving, on shipwrecks spanning five centuries of maritime history.
Top The wreck of the *Vixen*, a popular destination for glass-bottomed boats, is a favourite among divers.

Constellation and Nola Wrecks

The furthest reefs out to the northwest of Bermuda are the location of the two wrecks that inspired Peter Benchley's book *The Deep*, the film adaptation of which was largely made in Bermuda. The older of the two wrecks was thought to be the *Montana*, but is in fact the paddle steamer *Nola*. The other is the *Constellation*, a World War II supply ship that sank in 1943 while carrying, among other things, medical supplies.

The Intercontinental Steam Ship Company bought the *Constellation* and she began operating out of New York. In 1942, at the start of hostilities in World War II, the demand for ships grew even more urgent. The *Constellation* was drafted into Naval service and was converted back into a cargo ship. She carried a cargo weighing over 2000 tons, consisting of thousands of bags of cement; 700 cases of Scotch whisky; sheets of plate glass; slate; yo-yos; lead crucifixes; coffee cups; ceramic tiles; thousands of bottles containing everything from nail polish to mineral water; barrels of cold cream; and also 400,000 drug ampoules which included adrenaline, anti-tetanus serum, opium, morphine, and penicillin.

On 30 July 1943, while waiting for a pilot to steer her through the treacherous Bermudian reefs to the Royal Naval Dockyard on Ireland Island, she was caught in a powerful current and swept onto the reefs before the pilot could board her. The *Constellation* was lost, but the US Navy managed to salvage some of her cargo including – funnily enough – the 700 cases of whisky.

The reefs where she struck, in the vicinity of the Western Blue Cut, are particularly renowned for their treachery and, in fact, the *Constellation* sank only 15m (50ft) away from another much older ship, the *Nola*. This was an American Civil War blockade runner and was destroyed in 1863 in very similar conditions to those of the *Constellation*. Now the *Nola* rests in three pieces with her bow relatively intact, although partly collapsed. The paddle wheels, though encrusted in marine growth, are easily discernible, as are

Left The superstructure of the *Hermes* is a popular photographic subject for divers visiting Bermuda.

the forward boiler, anchor chain and chimney stack. Both these wrecks can be visited on a single dive. The *Constellation* is easily found as she is marked by a huge mound of cement bags, now turned to stone. Under the wreck can be found the remains of several thousand broken medicine bottles, including some of the fabled drug ampoules. There are very few fish in this area, as there is little coral growth.

for protection, and form a swirling mass that remains at arm's length from the diver. The perimeter of the shoal has barracuda, trumpetfish, jacks and sand divers, waiting to pick off prey.

The cave itself is home to spiny lobsters, cleaning shrimps and some delicately coloured sponges. As much of the swim-through is in the dark, or near dark, it is advisable to carry a dive light to be able to explore all of the recesses.

Eastern Blue Cut

Situated along the western reefs of Bermuda, the Eastern Blue Cut is the inside passageway through the treacherous reefs that have claimed so many ships, including the *Constellation*, the *Nola* and the *Lartington*, a steamship sunk in 1878 during a hurricane. Named after the deep sand patch in the reef, which reflects a light blue up to the surface, the reef to the right-hand side is deeply convoluted with some really superb caves and swim-throughs in the pristine coral reef.

It is fair to say that although Bermuda is not known for the proliferation of its fish life, most divers report seeing more fish on this reef than in any other area. The sand chute has some very large hogfish (*Lachnolaimus maximus*) and puddingwife (*Halichoeres radiatus*). A cut in the reef nearby always has a continuous stream of queen parrotfish (*Scarus vetula*) and the largest section of the reef has a massive tunnel cutting through it; in summer it is home to a huge shoal of silverside minnows. These are juveniles of a number of fish species which group together

Flatts Bridge

Flatts Bridge is at the entrance to Harrington Sound and has been singled out for the superb shore diving it offers. Two-and-a-quarter hours after high and low tide is slack water, when you may have up to 20 minutes of relative calm. The best way to approach this dive is to spend some time snorkelling on the periphery of the tidal race before slack water, where you can see tube worms, crabs, anemones, shrimps and lobsters in the shallows. The channel under the bridge is quite shallow and tapers off into the yacht marina on the outside.

The bottom here is littered with bottles, some dating back hundreds of years and almost all completely encrusted in a film of fire coral. However, on the inside of the channel a drop to 12m (40ft) is cut into the limestone wall and undercut by a ledge almost horseshoe in shape, which frames the entrance to the sound. Here is the rare green moray eel (*Gymnothorax funebris*) and quite possibly the largest spiny lobster ever seen (*Panulirus argus*). It is small wonder that you

see so many fish as the whole of Harrington Sound is a conservation area. The wealth of marine life probably encompasses virtually all of the species found around the islands.

The rich biodiversity of this site is reinforced by the fact that the Bermuda Aquarium is also situated at Flatts Bridge. It is interesting to make a comparison between those species in aquaria and those in their natural habitat only a five-minute walk away. The only rule that applies to diving at this location is to ask permission at the aquarium first. Also be aware of fishing boats and small passenger craft, which constantly move in and out of the Sound, particularly the research boats attached to the aquarium and the Marine Biological Centre.

Above right The paddle steamer *Nola* was a former confederate blockade runner, destroyed in 1863.

Left The ribs of the *Lartington* are now completely exposed to the elements near the Eastern Blue Cut.

Right Thousands of cement bags mark the position of the *Constellation* — these and a cargo of drug-filled ampoules were the inspiration for *The Deep*.

Atoll

Formed when an island submerges and the fringing coral reef grows upwards with the rise of the sea towards the light, forming a ring of coral.

Barrier Reef

An offshore reef that acts as a barrier, protecting the land from storms. It has a sand plain and patch reef between it and the shore.

Blow hole

Where wave and tidal action has eroded a hole in the ironstone shore and the waves create a huge plume of water that spurts out through the hole.

Buttress

A coral spur extending into the sea, normally from a reef wall or deep spur-and-groove reef.

Canyon

A slice in a coral reef or between granite boulders.

Chimney

Generally a narrow tunnel running vertically up through the edge of the outer reef.

Fringing Reef

A reef that is attached to the shore.

Ironstone shore

The petrified ancient coral reef that forms the base of a coral island.

Pinnacle or bommie

A large, tower-shaped coral head, separate from the main reef system; sometimes also referred to as a patch reef.

Sand chute

A deep gulley connecting the sand plain above the reef to the depths below. This only occurs in very deep waters and slopes off the edge of the continental shelf.

Shelf

Where the deep water begins.

Spur-and-groove reef

Coral spurs lie perpendicular to the shore, separated by sand and coral rubble chutes that have been carved through the coral reef by centuries of prevailing wave and weather action.

Tunnel

Sometimes known as a swim-through, ravine or crevice, this is a hole running through the reef or under granite rock.

Wall or drop-off

The side of a reef forming a shelf, a mini-wall that is the side of a stepped section of coral, or the side of a rocky vertical boulder.

Anguilla Tourist Office
Old Factory Plaza
PO Box 1388
The Valley
Anguilla
West Indies
Tel: (264) 497 2759
Fax: (264) 497 2710

Antigua and Barbuda Ministry of Tourism,
Culture and Environment
PO Box 363
St John's
Antigua
West Indies
Tel: (268) 462 0480
Fax: (268) 462 2483

Aruba Tourism Authority
LG Smith Boulevard
PO Box 1019
Oranjestad
Aruba
Dutch Antilles
Tel: (297) 82 37 77
Fax: (297) 83 47 02

Bahamas Ministry of Tourism
Market Plaza
PO Box N3701
Nassau, Bahamas
Tel: (242) 322 7500
Fax: (242) 322 4041

Barbados Department of Tourism
PO Box 242
Harbour Road
Bridgetown
Barbados
West Indies
Tel: (246) 427 2623
Fax: (246) 426 4080

Belize Tourist Board
83 North Front Street
Belize City
Belize
Tel: (501) 2 77213
Fax: (501) 2 77490

Bermuda Department of Tourism
Global House
43 Church Street
Hamilton HM 12
Bermuda
Tel: (441) 292 0023
Fax: (441) 292 7537

Bonaire Tourism Corporation
Kaya Libertador Simon Bolivar 12
Kralendijk, Bonaire
Dutch Antilles
Tel: (599 7) 8322
Fax: (599 7) 8408

British Virgin Islands Tourism Department
Social Security Building
Waterfront Street
PO Box 134
Road Town
Tortola
British Virgin Islands
Tel: (284) 494 3134
Fax: (284) 494 3866

Cayman Islands Department of Tourism
The Pavilion, Cricket Square
PO Box 67
Georgetown
Grand Cayman Island
Tel: 1 800 346 3313
Tel: (345) 949 0623
Fax: (345) 949 4053

Cuba National Institute of Tourism
Cuidad de la Habana
Habana
Cuba
Tel: (537) 32 05 70
Fax: (537) 33 40 86

Curaçao Tourism Development Bureau
Pietermaai 19
PO Box 3266
Willemstad
Curaçao
Dutch Antilles
Tel: (599 9) 616000
Fax: (599 9) 612305

Dominica Division of Tourism
PO Box 73
Roseau
Dominica
West Indies
Tel: (767) 448 2351
Fax: (767) 448 5840

Dominican Republic Ministry of Tourism
Av. Mexicosq. 30 de Marzo
Santo Domingo
Dominican Republic
Tel: (809) 221 4660
Fax: (809) 682 3806

Florida Keys and Key West Tourism Bureau
3406 North Roosevelt Boulevard
Suite 201
PO Box 201
Key West
Florida
SL3304T
USA
Tel: (305) 296 1552
Fax: (305) 296 0788

Grenada Department of Tourism
Burns Point
St George's
Grenada
West Indies
Tel: (473) 440 2279
Fax: (473) 440 6637

Guadeloupe Office Départemental du Tourisme
5 Square de la Banque
97110 Pointe-à-Pitre
Guadeloupe
French Antilles
Tel: (590) 82 09 30
Fax: (590) 83 89 22

Guyana Ministry of Trade,
Tourism and Industry
Main and Urquart Street
Georgetown
Guyana
Tel: (592) 26 53 84
Fax: (592) 25 43 10

Haiti Secretariat D'Etat Au Tourisme

8 Rue Légitime

Port-au-Prince

Haiti

Tel: (509) 23 56 31

Fax: (509) 23 53 39

Instituto Hondureno de Tourismo

Apdo. Postal 3261

Republica de Honduras

Centro America

Tel: (504) 22 2124

Fax: (504) 38 2102

Jamaica Department of Tourism

2 St Lucia Avenue

PO Box 360

Kingston 5

Jamaica

West Indies

Tel: (876) 929 9200

Fax: (876) 929 9375

Martinique Maison du Tourisme Vert

9 Bld du Général de Gaulle

BP 491

97205 Fort-de-France

Martinique

French Antilles

Tel: (596) 63 18 54

Fax: (596) 63 20 67

Mexico Tourism Promotion Office

PO Box 1339

Ignacia Garcia Avenue

Cancún

Quintana Roo

Mexico

77500

Tel: (00 52) 98 84 2853

Fax: (00 52) 98 84 7115

Montserrat Tourism Board

PO Box 7

Plymouth

Montserrat

West Indies

Tel: (664) 491 2230

Fax: (664) 491 7430

Puerto Rico Department of Economic Development and Commerce

355 Roosevelt Avenue

00918 Hato Rey

Puerto Rico

Tel: (787) 721 2400

Fax: (787) 725 4417

Saba Tourist Bureau

PO Box 527

Windwardside

Saba

Dutch Antilles

Tel: (599) 4 62231

Fax: (599) 4 62350

St Eustatius Tourist Bureau

Oranjestad

St Eustatius

Dutch Antilles

Tel: (599) 38 22 09

Fax: (599) 38 24 33

St Kitts and Nevis Ministry of Tourism, Culture and Environment

Pelican Mall

PO Box 132

Basseterre

St Kitts

West Indies

Tel: (869) 465 2620

Fax: (869) 465 8794

St Lucia Tourist Board

PO Box 221

Castries

St Lucia

West Indies

Tel (758) 452 4094

Fax (758) 453 1121

Sint Maarten Tourist Office

Walter Nisbeth Road

23 Philipsburg

Sint Maarten

Dutch Antilles

Tel: (599) 522 337

Fax: (599) 522 734

St Martin Office du Tourisme

Bld de France

Front de Mer

Marigot

St Martin

French Antilles

Tel: (590) 87 57 21

Fax: (590) 87 56 43

St Vincent and the Grenadines Tourism Office

PO Box 834

Bay Street

Kingstown

St Vincent

West Indies

Tel: (809) 457 1502

Fax: (809) 456 2610

Tourism and Industrial Development Company of Trinidad and Tobago Limited

Unit 12

IDC Mall

Sangster's Hill

Scarborough

Tobago

West Indies

Tel: (868) 639 4333

Fax: (868) 639 4514

Turks and Caicos Tourist Board

PO Box 128

Pond Street

Grand Turk

Turks and Caicos

Tel: (649) 946 2321

Fax: (649) 946 2733

United States Virgin Islands Division of Tourism

PO Box 6400

Charlotte Amalie

St Thomas

00804

Tel: (340) 774 8784

Fax: (340) 774 4390

Copyright in photography is held by the following photographers and/or their agents:

ACKNOWLEDGEMENTS

This book is dedicated to my wife Lesley, who only learned to dive in 1992 and then only to see for herself the wonderful creatures and the colours of the ocean that I was photographing. She has grown to love our underwater world and now, many hundreds of dives later, Lesley is not only my partner and diving buddy, she is also the strength and encouragement behind my passion. I have also received very specialized help from many individuals and tourist boards. Special thanks must go to Mariëlle Renssen, Thea Grobbelaar and Trinity Fry at

Park; Alain Capucci of the Miami International Airport Hotel; Michael and Karyn Allard of Scuba St Lucia and Anse Chastanet on St Lucia; Nick Davies and Jack Chalk at Captain Don's Habitat on Bonaire, as well as Lily-Anne Stewart, Michael, Marion Wilson and Jerry Schnabel. I thank Julie Angove and Cleveland Williams of the Bahamas Tourist Board; Rob Palmer and Steffie Schwabe of Rob Palmer's Blue Holes Foundation; Chris Allen at the Dolphin Experience; Ollie Ferguson and UNEXSO; Stuart Cove and the South Ocean

Struik International; Charlotte Parry-Crooke at New Holland; Steve Powell; Marion Porter; Sarah Leighton; Catherine Leech and Angela Martins of the Cayman Islands Tourist Board; Linton Tibbetts at the Brac Reef Resort; Sarah Wallace of the Caribbean Tourist Office; Alicia Cook at BGB Associates; Dierdre Keegan at Axis Management; Robert Ward at Harlequin Travel; Wayne and Anne Hasson of the Aggressor Fleet International and the many and varied crews on the *Cayman Aggressor III* and the *Bay Islands Aggressor III*; Liz Lower and Christine Taylor for Tobago and the Turks and Caicos tourist offices. Also on Tobago, thanks to Reginald Maclean and the Blue Waters Inn, Aquamarine Diving, Sean Robinson and Manta Lodge, Tobago Diving Experience, Man Friday Diving, Arnos Vale Hotel, and R&C Divers Den. In the Turks and Caicos, thanks to Club Med, Turtle Cove Inn, Provo Turtle Divers, Turtle Inn Divers, JoJo and Dean Bernal, Bill Clare and Capt' Bob Gascoine. In Cuba, Gaynor Power and Jorge Perez; Esther Smith and Dianelle Taylor at the St Kitts and Nevis Tourist Board; also on St Kitts: Austin McCleod, Pro Divers, Kenneth's Dive Centre, and Neil Goodwin at Horizon Villas Resort; and on Nevis: the Nisbet Plantation Club, Old Manor Estate and Hotel, Ajit Simha at the Oualie Beach Hotel, and Ellis Chaderton, Underwater Safaris. On Antigua, John Birk of Dive Antigua; Dave Martin and Ken Seed of Octopus Divers; Alex Zukrowski at the Long Bay Dive Shop; the Rex Halcyon Cove and Annette Michael of the Antigua Ministry of Tourism, Culture and Environment. On St Martin, I thank Dominique and LeRoy French at the Ocean Explorer Dive Centre; Saba Marine

Club; Steven Frink; Ana Lara Aguilar, Director of the Mexican Tourist Board in London; Steve Gerrard; Tony and Nancy DeRosa; Mike Madden and Luis Gomez; Quicksilver Cancun; Manta Divers; Rene Applegate at Dive Paradise; Dive House; the Fiesta Americana Cozumel Reef Hotel; Alan Marquardt; Michael Burke from Blue Water Divers; Charlie Green from Nautilus Diving Ltd; Michael Heslop from Fantasea Diving; Tony Stewart from South Side Scuba; Harry Soares of Scuba Look; Lanatana Colony Club; Greenbank Guesthouse; Longtail Cliffs and Cambridge Beaches – all in Bermuda and supported by Charles Green and Pippa Grive from the Bermuda Tourist Offices – and Coral Cay Conservation in Belize. On Curaçao, All West Diving and Apartments; Chernov; Underwater Curaçao; Lions Dive Hotel and Marina, and the Curaçao Seaquarium. Thanks to Christine Oliver of the British Virgin Islands Tourist Office; Kilbrides Underwater Tours at the Bitter End Yacht Club; Dive BVI from Leverick Bay; Baskin In The Sun; Prospect Reef Resort; Nanny Cay; Blue Water Divers; Underwater Safaris; Treasure Isle Hotel and the superb *Cuan Law* operated by the Trimarine Boat Co Ltd. In the United States Virgin Islands, my thanks go to Jenny Spurgeon; Waves at Cane Bay; VI Divers; Chris Sawyer and Low Key Watersports. I also thank Liat, Winair, BWIA, Virgin Atlantic, British Airways, Caledonian Airways, Caribbean Airways, and SkyKing. Finally my thanks go to KJP of Edinburgh; Fuji; Tamron Lenses; Sea and Sea of Paignton in Devon, England; Nikon UK Ltd; The Shark Group of Amble in Northumberland, England; and Eastern Photocolour in Edinburgh.